EXPLORE
EDINBURGH

THE CITY, ITS HERITAGE AND COUNTRYSIDE

VALERIE GREEN

COUNTRYSIDE BOOKS

EXPLORE EDINBURGH
The City, Its Heritage and Countryside
by Valerie Green

First published 1988
© Valerie Green

COUNTRYSIDE BOOKS
3 Catherine Road,
Newbury, Berkshire

Produced through
MRM Associates, Reading, Berkshire
Cover Photographs by Andy Williams
Typeset by Acorn Bookwork, Salisbury
Printed in England

ISBN 1 85306 003 8

BIBLIOGRAPHY

Barclay, J. B. *Edinburgh*
Birrell, Dr J. F. *An Edinburgh Alphabet*
Catford, E. F. *Edinburgh, Story of a City*
Gillespie, T. H. *The Story of Edinburgh Zoo*
Hamilton, A. *Essential Edinburgh*
Slavin, K. & J. *Around Scotland*
Tranter, N. *The Lothians*
Tranter, N. *Fortified Houses*
Old and New Edinburgh
Concise Dictionary of National Biographies
Edinburgh – Capital City

ACKNOWLEDGEMENTS

My very special gratitude goes to my husband,
Ronnie, to whom this book is dedicated, for his
whole-hearted encouragement, endless copy
reading and support throughout the months of its
preparation.

Grateful thanks, too, to Dr J. F. Birrell who so
kindly allowed me to make use of his own
research findings; and Russell Eberst who
contributed the article on the Royal Observatory.

Many organisations and individuals have also
given unstinted co-operation: The Marquess of
Linlithgow, the Earl and Countess of Rosebery,
the staff of Edinburgh District Council, Royal
Zoological Society of Scotland, Edinburgh
Tapestry Co. Ltd., Leith Project, Forth Ports
Authority, National Trust for Scotland, Scotmid
Co-operative Society, National Art Galleries of
Scotland, National Museums of Scotland,
Scottish Steam Railway Preservation Society,
Countryside Rangers Association, Scottish
Borders Tourist Board, Roxburgh District
Council, and the Music Faculty of Edinburgh
University. Thanks also to Val Dean, Jean
Crichton, Douglas Russell, Jim Quinn, Jean
Thompson, Paul Vallot, and many others who
gave me the benefit of their knowledge and
supplied photographs. My thanks to everyone.

Valerie Green

The concept of this book was developed from
EXPLORE HAMPSHIRE, published by Hampshire
County Council Recreation Department, to whom
the publishers offer a grateful acknowledgement.

CONTENTS

Maps and Street Plans

Brief directions as to the location of each attraction are given with the text in this book. However, *Explore Edinburgh* covers not only the city itself but also much of the surrounding countryside (see area map above). Those using the book will therefore find it valuable to purchase a simple street plan of Edinburgh city and make use of a road atlas to a scale of approximately four miles to the inch. The 1 : 50,000 and 1 : 25,000 Ordnance Survey maps of the area are also recommended.

Information on bus routes and times may be obtained from the following:

Lothian Region Transport (covering the city)
14 Queen Street   Edinburgh
Tel: 031 554 4494

Eastern Scottish (outside the city)
St Andrew Square Bus Station   Edinburgh
Tel: 031 556 8464

The 'price guide' given for some of the attractions is simply a guide to the cost of entry.

Cost for one adult:
A: under 50p
B: 50p–£1
C: £1–£2
D: £2–£3
E: £3–£4

Prices may change in the future but the guides should remain a useful pointer to which are relatively dear and which are relatively cheap. As the most expensive sites offer a complete day out with special attractions, the classification is no indication of value for money.

Visitors are advised to check all entrance fees and opening times in advance to avoid disappointment.

INTRODUCTION

The number of books which have been written about Edinburgh is almost overwhelming, and range from multi-volume historical tomes to pocket guides. *Explore Edinburgh* does not attempt to emulate them. It is intended as a fresh look at what Scotland's capital city and its environs have to offer residents and visitors, bringing back to mind places practically on the doorstep which, simply because they are there, have merged into the landscape and are frequently overlooked.

It is an accepted fact that the people who live in a town or city are often those who know least about it. Or perhaps their knowledge is based on a flurry of sightseeing ten or twenty years ago, and since then the face of the city has changed, with buildings knocked down or altered. Indeed, even since this book went into print, someone in Edinburgh is sure to have moved something somewhere else – it has been a popular pastime in recent years.

The author came to live in Edinburgh twenty two years ago, and did the statutory sightseeing tour shortly afterwards. It wasn't until *Explore Edinburgh* was being written – a task which involved plodding round virtually every location mentioned – that the changes which had been made became apparent, and also just how perfunctory is most people's idea of sightseeing in their own area when, metaphorically speaking, the next bend in the road would have revealed yet another place to explore. Perhaps a stately home; a unique collection of keyboard instruments or old transport; a working water mill; or a

prehistoric burial mound. They are all there, and much more, waiting to welcome those who can tear themselves away from the television set and go out into the world.

One of the problems about *Explore Edinburgh* was not so much what to put in, but what to leave out! The main concern within these pages is with the Edinburgh of today, where to go and what to see; to cater for all generations and interests; and to enjoy the folklore and legends which creep in here and there.

This will be no history book – the author is happy to leave that in the more competent hands of the ardent student. Nevertheless, a little history will help the reader appreciate the very basis of Edinburgh's being.

If one's brain can grasp the enormity of time in millions of years, then we have to go back that far to find the geological beginnings of today's landscape, when great eruptions pushed up the seven volcanic plugs on which the city is built. Years later, Ice Age glaciers grinding their way from west to east moulded the gentle curves of the Pentlands, and carved the deep troughs around the Castle Rock and nearby Arthur's Seat.

No-one knows when man first decided that the Castle Rock, surrounded by forests and lochs, would make a good home, although prehistoric man has left traces of his habitations throughout the area. The Romans, when they came, displayed little interest in the Castle Rock; their sights were set on the whole of Scotland as an extension of the Roman Empire, but after a

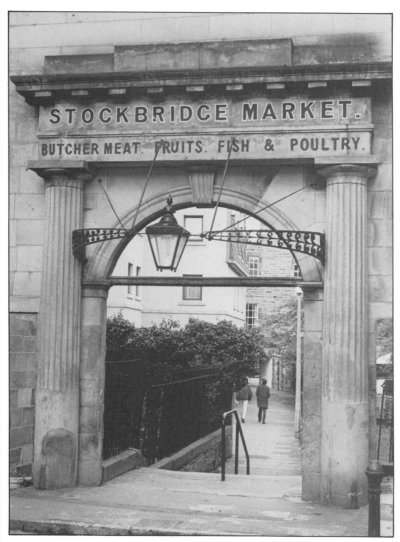

capital. With a royal presence firmly established, the little town which had grown up under the protection of the castle walls continued to develop and prosper, and in 1329 King Robert the Bruce extended the royal burgh to take in the seaport of Leith and the milling centre of Dean Village.

Donaldson's School for the deaf

The 1400s saw the start of 250 years of turbulence for the Scottish people – almost continuous warfare with the English; the sometimes erratic life-style of the thrice-wed Mary, Queen of Scots; strife between religious factions resulting in bloodshed among the Scots themselves; the great plague of 1645 which swept through the Old Town; and the ill-fated Jacobite risings.

As peace returned, it had become increasingly obvious that the Old Town could no longer contain its overflowing population, and proposals

Liberton Church whose tower was used as a beacon for shipping

few futile attempts they were pushed back over Hadrian's Wall and eventually out of Britain altogether.

We have to wait until the late eleventh century before anything reasonably tangible is agreed by the historians, for it was during these years that Malcolm III and his Queen Margaret moved from their Dunfermline home to take the Scottish capital to Edinburgh.

The next monarch of any consequence was Malcolm's fourth son, David I, who after his accession in 1124 was to make such an impact in monastic circles with his founding of Holyrood and the great abbeys of the Border towns. All of these were destined to suffer devastating attacks from Hertford's English troops during the invasions of the mid-1500s.

And what of Edinburgh while David was having his abbeys built? It appears from extracts of charters granting Royal Burgh status to many embryo towns that David was most certainly king of his castle, and his declaration that it should become a permanent royal residence effectively ensured the continuity of Edinburgh as Scotland's

Interior of Georgian House

furnished rooms as they may have been in the days of the first owners, faithfully reconstructing the domestic surroundings to reflect the social conditions of the age.

The Nor' Loch, now Princes Street Gardens, had been partially drained for the foundations of the original North Bridge between the Old and New Towns. The other link was The Mound, which more or less built itself. Originally a quagmire left by the half-drained loch, it became known as Geordie Boyd's Mud Brig after one George Boyd, a tailor, used it as a short cut. An obvious place to dump the accumulation of earth displaced by digging the foundations of the New Town, The Mound was estimated to contain two million cartloads by the time the steeply-sloping road was finished in 1830.

As the streets were systematically completed, so began the steady exodus of the gentry, the upper and middle classes, from the confines of the Old Town to the fresher pastures of the New. The houses planned by Craig were soon filled, and the city of Edinburgh continued to expand with the building of the many crescents and elegant terraces so reminiscent of Bath, presenting a miscellany of architectural faces acquired over the years from the oldest restorations in the Royal Mile to the present-day suburban spread which has absorbed the surrounding villages.

And yet, despite its expansion, Edinburgh has managed to retain a certain compactness, even outlying suburbs being barely half-an-hour's bus run from the throbbing pulse of Princes Street. There are few cities, let alone capital cities, which can make that boast.

were made to build a New Town to the north of the castle ridge. Architect James Craig was awarded the task of drawing up the plans, and his ideas were geometrically simple.

Building of this Georgian New Town began in 1767, and the long ruler–straight roads of Princes Street, George Street and Queen Street, intersected equally neatly by Castle Street, Frederick Street, Hanover Street, and St David Street, culminate tidily with the elegant buildings of Charlotte Square and St Andrew Square to complete a grid-iron pattern.

View from Blackford Hill

If one can ignore the parking meters surrounding the private central garden in Charlotte Square, little has been allowed to change. Front doors, fan-lights and windows must conform to their original design, and the only concession on the elegant lamps was the switch to electricity.

Fittingly enough, the official residence of the Secretary of State for Scotland is here. So, too, are the head offices of the National Trust for Scotland, who some years ago presented a flashback in time with the opening of the adjoining Georgian House, at No. 7. Here, the Trust have

Waverley Station with Scott Monument in background

Modern Edinburgh does not, however, sit back sedately content with past achievements. One has only to count the number of theatres, concert halls, cinemas, discos, museums, art galleries – yes, and restaurants of many nations as well – to realise why the city rarely seems to sleep.

Throughout the year, there is always so much to do, whatever one's interests. It could be a performance from a visiting overseas company; traditional Scots music and verse; an exhibition; or just sampling the mysteries of strange cuisine.

The green-domed Usher Hall, built in 1913 with £10,000 gifted by Sir John Usher, is the major classical concert venue where the Scottish National Orchestra gives regular performances, although its doors have been opened for such lighter entertainment as James Last and his orchestra. The much smaller Queen's Hall in Clerk Street includes in its calendar concerts by local orchestral groups, catering for a musical spectrum through classics to the occasional pop. St Giles Cathedral and St John's Church on Princes Street offer choral recitals; and lunchtime concerts at the Assembly Rooms in George Street and St Cecelia's Hall in the Cowgate provide welcome breaks in a working day.

Waverley Market Cafe

Lovers of live theatre can hardly ask for more variety than that offered by the King's Theatre. Scottish Opera and Scottish Ballet productions intermingle with modern plays, musicals, or 'Mesdames' Hinge and Bracket, with the ever-popular pantomime taking over on its Christmas cue. As well as the King's, theatregoers have the choice of the Royal Lyceum, The Traverse, Church Hill, and others, all well publicised.

The annual highlight of Edinburgh's cultural activities is, of course, the International Festival held every August, when thousands of visitors from all over the world converge on the city as spectators or participants in all branches of the arts – music, films, drama, dance, jazz, mime – the list is endless. The growth of The Fringe and its more off-beat productions in recent years means that not only are the city's concert halls and theatres filled to capacity, but so too is every obscure nook and cranny able to accommodate a few chairs as well as the performers.

Wax Museum on the Royal Mile

The three-week Festival, which has earned Edinburgh the tag of Festival City, was started in the bleak post-war autumn of 1947, and has been held ever more impressively as each year passes. The biggest single attraction is the Military Tattoo staged by Scottish Command on the Castle Esplanade with the floodlit castle as its backdrop. Such a setting could not be more appropriate. The Castle Rock was the birthplace of Edinburgh, and with its great battlements and St Margaret's tiny chapel outlined against the night sky, it has survived the test of time and remains the very core of Scotland's capital city.

The Forth Rail Bridge

Ramsay Gardens

SOUTH QUEENSFERRY

Thousands of visitors from all over the world descend on South Queensferry each year to gaze at the view of the Forth's two magnificent bridges opposite the sixteenth-century Hawes Inn. Those who take the trouble to walk along the seafront and into the town are rewarded with a jump back in time.

Another hotel, perched precariously high on a rocky outcrop which was once a playground for seals, marks the start of the narrow main street which curves its way through the town, trapped on either side by an array of many-hued houses – some dating back to the 1600s – creating an architectural cocktail which is quaint, yet curiously palatable.

The Black Castle

To find the main street terraced on two levels is unusual, too. In the days before bulldozers, it was the logical answer to the problem of building up a hillside rising sharply from The Binks, the rocky shelves fringing the estuary.

The solid houses include the sombre Black Castle of 1626, which still wears its original livery, and the more lightly-named Laburnum House of the same era, once homes of the gentry, merchants and burgesses of South Queensferry. Even earlier inhabitants were the Carmelite monks, into whose fifteenth-century monastery was incorporated the later Priory Church.

There is the Tolbooth with its clock tower; the well presented by Lord Rosebery in 1817 to bring the first public water supply to the village; and Plewlands House which dominated the old market place.

NORTH QUEENSFERRY

North Queensferry, once so important as the crossing point for the Forth, is now largely overlooked by visitors. Nevertheless it is an interesting village. Stop for a few minutes near the old ferry landing. Here you will find North Queensferry's most poignant monument – a six-sided stone tower built in about 1810, which originally housed the light kept burning to guide ships to the old pier at night. Supports for the firebasket are still fixed on the ground floor, while the flue shaft goes through the internal spiral stone stair to the glazed lamphouse above.

In the village itself is the Waterloo Memorial, a bell-shaped font erected round the old village well in 1816. It was here that horses were watered and stagecoaches washed down before continuing what was probably a tedious journey, and it is unlikely to be sheer chance that there is a hostelry across the road!

Behind and close by the memorial is the old village pump itself, and camouflaging the mechanism of the water supply is an intriguing worked iron plaque. Apparently it was a regular occurrence for ships anchored nearby to send ashore a crewman under cover of darkness to steal water for replenishing the ship. The plaque depicts a cross-faced woman scolding and belabouring a cowering sailorman, whose luck had obviously run dry on that occasion.

The village pump

THE TALE OF TWO BRIDGES

Roads of a sort have linked main settlements since time began, but the Firth of Forth was always an impassable water barrier for travellers, unless the local boatmen could be persuaded to make the crossing in exchange for a few pieces of silver.

The saintly Queen Margaret, the wife of Malcolm III who was canonised after her death, was so scandalised by these demands that, in the latter part of the eleventh century, she made a grant enabling pilgrims travelling to and from the religious centre at St Andrews to cross free of charge. The fact that she herself often wished to cross the Forth may have had something to do with it.

The increasing need to move between towns on either side of the estuary meant the introduction of bigger and better boats, and later still ferries which could carry stage-coaches as well as foot travellers. The crossing became known as the Queensferry Passage, linking the north and south side villages which also took her name, and it continued to provide a water-borne service for 900 years.

Although tentative plans for a road bridge were first proposed as far back as 1740, it was to be more than 200 years before the long-sought-after project got under way.

In the interim, the development of the railway had far outstripped that of road transport, and the powerful railway hierarchy was not slow to realise its potential as a major carrier of human and freight cargo.

The Forth Rail Bridge, designed by Sir John Fowler and Benjamin Baker

As the railways spread north through Scotland along the east coast, one frustrating barrier lay ahead: the Firth of Forth. And so long as this obstacle remained unsurmounted, the railway chiefs in the east suffered the constant threat of their competitors in the west encroaching on what they regarded as 'their' territory north of the river. One must remember that in those early days of steam, the whole of Britain was covered by rail networks operated by individual companies, not always averse to a bit of poaching here and there.

So the most ambitious plan of all was hatched; to bridge the gap with the most colossal structure of its kind that man's brains and skills could achieve.

In 1873, the foundation stone for a suspension bridge designed by engineer Thomas Bouch was placed in position by his wife. This would be his second mammoth bridge undertaking, even longer than his first – the ill-fated Tay Bridge which was destined to collapse into the Tay estuary during a storm in December 1879, carrying with it the Edinburgh train and killing more than 70 passengers.

Following this disaster, work immediately stopped on the Forth bridge, but within a year the four railway companies concerned in the project, the Great Northern, the North Eastern, the Midland and the North British, announced their intention of going ahead with a re-designed structure.

More plans were submitted, and early in 1883 work began, this time on the much stronger principle of a steel-girdered cantilever bridge, designed by Sir John Fowler and Benjamin Baker.

Memories of the Tay disaster were too recent to allow for any errors, and throughout the building operations tests were continually carried out to check the stress of moving trains and their loads, tidal action, and the particular hazard of excessive wind pressure which was held partly responsible for the collapse of the Tay bridge.

It says much for the designers that, because of the care they took to ensure that each part of the structure was totally secure before moving on to the next stage, only 57 men lost their lives in the seven-year project which involved extensive work below sea level and also at great heights. The death toll could have been higher from accidental falls into the water had it not been for the rescue rowing boats stationed at the foot of each cantilever.

Of the men themselves, the majority were Scots, English or Irish, although the workforce at times included labourers brought over from Europe.

In November 1889, the bridge was completed with the closing of the final gap in the massive

The Forth Rail Bridge

tracery of girders which soar 360 feet above high water mark, cost three million pounds to construct, stretches for more than one and a half miles, and now carries some 200 trains every 24 hours.

As well as the seven million rivets used, the last of which was driven home by the Prince of Wales when he opened the bridge in March 1890, the materials used included 54,000 tons of steel; 21,000 tons of cement; and 194,000 cubic yards of granite, stone and concrete. With a painting area of about 145 acres, more than 35,500 gallons of paint oils and 250 tons of paint were also used during construction.

According to popular belief, painting the Forth Rail Bridge from end to end is something which goes on all the time. Not so. Sections are repainted as required by the 16 men who dangle alarmingly over the estuary in their hydraulically-operated cradles as part of a regular six-year programme of general maintenance and cleaning.

From a miracle of Victorian engineering to an equally impressive miracle of twentieth century technology – this is the step between the chunky Forth Rail Bridge and its streamlined young sister, the Forth Road Bridge.

Originally thought of in the eighteenth century, the road bridge scheme was put to one side for nearly 75 years until an Edinburgh engineer produced plans for a chain bridge, only to have the idea shelved again with the upsurge of the railway. The battle for the bridge began in earnest in the 1920s, with meetings in Edinburgh, South Queensferry, and the House of Commons, where the Ministry of Transport eventually agreed to a survey.

Although a survey was submitted, covering three possible sites, the bridge was still a long way off. The nation's economic traumas squashed it in 1931 and again in 1934; World War II resulted in further postponement; and it took ten years from approval of the 1947 Forth Road Bridge Order before Government permission was given for work to start on this great suspension bridge.

The site having previously been agreed upon, those latter years were spent on detailed surveys and borings of the river and its approaches. Bridge designs and components were also thoroughly tested with the aid of computers and a wind tunnel somewhat more sophisticated than that used for the rail bridge.

The initial stage of construction was the building of the piers for the main towers, side towers, and cable anchorages, and to achieve this the bed of the estuary had to be penetrated to a depth of 100 feet in places to lay the foundations on the rock itself. High-tensile steel was used for the two 500-foot main towers which support the spectacular central span of 3,300 feet.

From the side towers the supporting cables disappear into their anchorages: massive wedges tunnelled into the rock. The main cables are made up of more than 11,000 strands, each the thickness of a pencil, and using enough wire to reach one and a quarter times round the Equator.

The Forth Road Bridge

Once these were in place, the work could go ahead of systematically placing the steel trusses supporting the road decking in the wire loops which hung down from the main cables. Now the bridge began to take shape, as cranes mounted on the main towers gradually eased the huge sections into place, reaching out over the water like probing fingers.

The day of reckoning came in December 1963, when the two halves met in the middle of the main span, and the gap was closed with only an inch or so to spare. Roadways, cycle tracks, and footpaths could now be completed, asphalt laid, lighting installed, and in the following year the 19½ million-pound bridge was officially opened by the Queen.

INCHCOLM ISLAND

St Colm's Abbey

One of the most satisfactory ways of really escaping from your fellow human beings for a couple of hours is to go and sit on an island, preferably in the sun, in the middle of the Firth of Forth, smug in the knowledge that you are quite cut off from the rat-race until the boatman decides it's time to go.

This retreat, just along the road – or estuary – is Inchcolm Island. It may appear on the map as only a tiny blob, but it is in fact large enough to absorb a boat-load of visitors so completely that it is easy to find a secluded spot.

Inchcolm must have been blessed with this atmosphere of serenity since time began, as its first inhabitants were a succession of hermits in the Dark Ages. One of these, St Colm, is regarded as the island's patron saint. Nothing much is known about him, except that he has been identified with St Columba, the sixth-century abbot of Iona.

The well-preserved remains of the monastery have been dated to 1123, when King Alexander I and some of his court, blown off-course in a storm while crossing the Forth, fortuitously managed to land at Inchcolm. In thanksgiving, he founded the priory in the saint's honour.

When King David I came to the throne, he gave the job of administering the new priory to the Bishop of Dunkeld, who also supervised the settlement of the Augustinian community on the island. Succeeding Bishops of Dunkeld continued to play an important role in the progress of St Colm's from priory to abbey, and many of them are buried on the island.

Inchcolm was not, however, able to stay aloof during the many years of war between the Scots and English, who on a number of occasions sent ships to plunder the defenceless island before some measure of fortification was built in about 1430. Despite the threat of raids, repair and extension work was still carried on and today's ruins show the variations in architecture over those years.

The Reformation in 1560 meant the virtual end of St Colm's as an abbey. No new canons were admitted, but the existing members of the order were allowed to remain as pensioners; the abbey ceased to be used for religious purposes in 1578.

But the island's usefulness did not end there. It was for some years a quarantine post for plague-carrying ships, and a hospital was provided there in the 1790s to serve the Russian Fleet lying in the Forth. Extra fortifications were built during the Napoleonic wars and First World War, to be utilised yet again by the army during the Second World War.

Such turbulent times are now far behind, but not forgotten. Restoration work has revealed the fascinating nooks and crannies of the picturesque octagonal chapter house and vaulted cloisters, the tower with its roof walk, and even the domestic quarters and hospital, surrounded now by carefully-manicured lawns and gravel paths.

Away from the abbey precincts, Inchcolm Island is in itself as nature intended it. Gentle hummocks too small to be called hills provide startling views of the Edinburgh and Fife coastlines over the waters of the Forth which lap against the tiny beaches and rocks of the island.

'MAID OF THE FORTH'

How to get there:
By car: A90 then B924 slip road to South Queensferry

By bus: From St. Andrew Square

Car parking: Free

Nearby attractions: Hopetoun House, Dalmeny House

The *Maid of the Forth*, despite the romantic name, is not some phantom damsel from the past, but a very business-like 35-ton motor vessel which is the only way to get to Inchcolm Island from South Queensferry unless you happen to be lucky enough to have your own yacht.

Owner and skipper of the spanking blue-and-white boat is locally-born John Watson, who in 1980 gave up his job as a civil servant to return to the sea and resurrect what was once a popular pastime in the Firth of Forth, that of short cruising trips. Inchcolm was the ideal port of call round which to plan these trips, and the boat passes many other places of interest on the river, about which John gives a running commentary.

Leaving from her base at Hawes Pier, which was the ferry terminal before the road bridge ended the service after 900 years, the *Maid* sails under the railway bridge with its massive cantilever towers. It is only at such close quarters that one realises how gigantic this feat of engineering was when it was tackled a hundred years ago.

Of much more recent vintage is the Hound Point oil terminal, visible evidence of the North Sea oil industry which has sprung up in recent years. The terminal on a man-made island handles crude oil pumped from the Forties Field, and exports on average eight million tons every year using some of the world's largest tankers.

On the south shore of the Forth can be seen the stark walls of Barnbougle Castle. Basically a seventeenth-century building with later restorations, the castle is part of the Rosebery estate but is not open to the public. Legend has it that a ghostly dog howls on nearby Hound Point when the death of the Laird of Barnbougle is imminent, a tale which dates from the Crusades when a laird and his dog both perished in the Holy Land.

'Maid of the Forth'

Over in Fife is Donibristle House, an historic mansion which was a centre of intrigue during the reign of Mary Tudor. An old ballad tells how the Earl of Moray was killed and his home sacked because he had attracted the interest of James V's wife.

The boat operates throughout the summer on a daily basis. The sailing time to Inchcolm is 25 minutes, and more than an hour is allowed ashore, giving a round trip of two hours. Evening cruises are non-landing, and offer one and a half hours of sailing. At other times of the year, the boat is much in demand for school parties, and it is also possible to charter her for private functions.

Fitted with radar to combat the treacherous *haar*, or sea mist, which can roll up the estuary with little warning, *Maid of the Forth* is a 56-foot, twin-screw vessel capable of ten knots. She can carry 100 passengers in covered accommodation, although the more hardy types may prefer to stay up on the observation deck. The pleasant saloon offers a small bar and light refreshments.

CRAMOND

How to get there:
By car: A90 to Barnton, turn right at double roundabout

Car parking: free

Nearby Attractions: Dalmeny House, Lauriston Castle

Price Guide: Free, but donations welcomed by Trust

Handicapped: Suitable

Publications: Available from Cramond Heritage Trust at The Maltings

Where to eat: Cramond Inn; cafe along promenade; Suitable picnic areas on promenade or beach

Public Transport: Bus service No. 41 from Princes Street via Davidsons Mains.

invaders, possibly because they provided a ready market for their farm produce and livestock. They were not to know that during the next 100 years or so the troops were to be repeatedly withdrawn from Scottish campaigning, then sent back. This intermittent occupation continued

Cramond, a delightfully picturesque village at the mouth of the river Almond, only minutes from the centre of Edinburgh, attracts visitors not just for its tranquility but also for the fascinating history of the site uncovered in recent years.

During the first Roman occupation of Scotland nearly 2000 years ago, some 500 engineers and infantrymen – thought to be from *II Legio Augusta* came, saw, and decided that Cramond would be the ideal place at which to build a fort as an outlier and supply depot for the 'Antonine Wall', which ended a few miles to the west on the Forth estuary.

The 'Wall', named after its originator, the Emperor Antoninus Pius, was planned as a forward frontier linking the Clyde with the Forth. Albeit a less enduring structure than the massive Hadrian's Wall in Northumberland, where at that time civilisation effectively stopped, it was an essential part of the emperor's ambition to push even further north, his troops establishing fortified depots as they advanced.

So the fort was built; a harbour was made to accommodate the ships bringing supplies from the south; and near the site there grew up a native village occupied by the local barbarian tribe.

The barbarians, known as the Votadini and for some obscure reason speaking an early form of Welsh, appeared to welcome the Roman

throughout the 'Second Antonine' era, and the campaigns of Emperor Septimius Severus, which were all of relatively short duration.

Although the existence of the fort at Cramond had been suspected for some time, the site was not actually discovered until 1954. It took 12 years of excavations to piece together the layout of Caer Amon (the 'Fort on the Almond') as it was then called.

Rectangular in shape, and facing the Forth and sea approaches to the estuary, the fort covered about six acres. Its stone-faced clay ramparts were 27 feet thick and estimated to be 20 feet high, punctuated by four gates flanked by towers, with possibly less sturdy towers at the rampart corners. In the centre of the fort area was the Headquarters, or *Principia*, which now forms the foundations of Cramond Church.

The thousands of artefacts found during the dig, from coins and jewellery to shards of pottery and glass, are housed at the Huntly Museum in the Royal Mile, Edinburgh, but there is a plan of the fort's layout beside the church.

The church has had a chequered career. The tower and east end are basically medieval, but much of the structure dates from the seventeenth century. Centuries of rebuilding, extension, and even major changes of devotional direction, have done little to alter the 1656 exterior, although the inside is relatively modern.

A short walk from the church is Cramond Tower, perched on high ground overlooking the Forth and surrounded by 300-year-old trees. There are varying opinions as to its origin, but some believe it to be part of the Summer Palace of the Bishops of Dunkeld, the Bishopric having been granted the lands of Cramond in the twelfth century by King David I.

In 1978, George Jamieson, a wildlife artist and taxidermist, acquired the tower and its grounds. It had been sadly neglected for more than 200 years, but once the screen of strangling ivy and other vegetation was cleared away, a classic example of a four-storey medieval defensive tower was revealed. In the course of intensive restoration work the pitched roof was replaced, masonry re-pointed, floors inserted, the spiral turnpike staircase largely replaced, and modern amenities installed so that once again it is a comfortable home. It is also 'home' for the exhibitions of his work which Mr Jamieson holds from time to time.

Nearby is Cramond House, a mansion built, in part, by the Lairds of Cramond in the 1680s. The classical back and front we see today were added later. The house was imposing enough to have attracted royal attention, for Queen Victoria is thought to have spent a holiday there.

Cramond Tower

As a reminder of the days when Cramond supported a small industry of water-powered iron mills, producing sheet- and rod-iron, nails and shovels between 1752 and 1860, workmen's houses – now modernised – still stand overlooking the river and the skeletons of the mills. These houses are easily spotted by the proliferation of chimney pots! Each family was allowed only one room of a house to live in, and as every room needed a hearth for cooking and heating, so each needed its own 'lum'.

Unfortunately, many other such houses were demolished in 1826 when Lady Torphichen, the then laird, saw fit to destroy half the village in order to 'improve' the estate by ensuring that the working population was kept further out of sight and mind!

Probably the most well-known building in the village is the 300-year-old Cramond Inn, once popular with Robert Louis Stevenson and just as popular today with its gleaming white walls, black paintwork, crow-stepped gables, and somewhat haphazard doors and windows.

From the river mouth, the wide promenade begins its long sweep eastwards along the estuary foreshore, and when the tide is out, one can walk across the causeway to Cramond Island, a favourite haunt of the many species of birds which inhabit this part of the coast.

If one is tempted by the green farmlands of Dalmeny Estate to the west, or the prospect of a longer walk to South Queensferry (five miles), the Cramond ferryman will obligingly pole visitors across the narrowing river for a modest fee.

All the places of interest in this compact, walk-about village are clearly marked, owing to the efforts of residents who formed themselves into the Cramond Association in an endeavour to preserve their heritage.

An offshoot of the Association is the Cramond Heritage Trust, which holds a permanent exhibition at The Maltings. Association members also organise Sunday guided tours during the summer months, and literature dealing with the 'rise and fall, and rise again' of the village is available at The Maltings.

CULROSS

National Trust for Scotland Properties

How to get there:
Cross Forth Road Bridge; take A985 westwards 12 miles:
Or M9 to slip road for Kincardine Bridge; A985 eastwards 4 miles

Car parking: Free park on West side of town

Open: Town House: May–September (except Friday) 9.30–12.30, 2.00–5.00; Sunday 2.00–5.00
The Study: April and October, Saturday 9.30–12.30, 2.00–4.00 Sunday 2.00–4.00
Or by prior appointment

Price Guide: C (Town House, Study, and audio-visual presentation)

Where to eat: Hotel, Tea Rooms

The history of Culross goes back to the sixth century. Then, it was an important religious centre, whose monks were responsible for the upbringing and education of the infant St Mungo, who was to become the patron saint of Glasgow. Nine hundred years later, a chapel to St Mungo was built by the first Archbishop of Glasgow on the hill behind Culross to mark his supposed birthplace, the ruins now gently softened by the surrounding garden.

In common with so many Scottish towns, Culross owed much of its sixteenth-century affluence to the local community of monks. It was they who realised the potential of coal and developed a thriving salt-panning enterprise. Their enthusiasm for coal mining waned as extraction problems increased. It needed the pioneering efforts of Sir George Bruce in the late 1500s to bring Culross colliery back to its previous prosperity, only to lose the entire undersea workings during a storm in 1625. This was the beginning of the end for the town's industries – ironwork, leather and shoe-making were inadequate substitutes.

Culross Palace

A permanent reminder of the halcyon years is Sir George's Palace, built in two stages as his importance grew, and the Trust's initial acquisition of 1932.

Fronting the estuary, whose waters at one time washed up to the shore road before land reclamation resulted in today's greensward, is the Town House. This was built in 1626, a new frontage and clock-tower being added in 1783. Its ground floor once served as a prison for witches and debtors, while the first floor rooms – now the Trust Centre – were the Council Chambers.

Mercat Cross

Turning away from the seafront, it is a fairly steep climb up the cobbles of the winding Back Causeway with its raised centre stones for the gentry to walk on, while lesser mortals had to step aside into the gutters. This leads to the oldest part of Culross, the Square, with its Mercat (market) Cross and crow-stepped gabled houses which many visitors find more appealing than the grander Palace.

The main building here is The Study, built around 1610, and so named because it was believed to have been used by Bishop Leighton of Dunblane when he stayed at Culross during his diocesan visits. Now the home of the Trust's local representative, the main room with its intricately painted and beamed ceiling may be seen by arrangement.

Leaving behind the town's oldest house, bearing the date 1577 on one gable, and continuing to climb, one passes three cottages which have been privately restored. So that there should have been no doubt in anyone's mind as to who lived where, they are respectively named Snuff Cottage, Coachman's Cottage, and the Tanhouse.

Dominating the town is the church, restored in 1633, and so closely does it adhere to the site of the Cistercian abbey founded by Malcolm in 1217, that its fabric incorporates the original west wall of the Lay Brothers' choir. The well-kept ruins of the abbey provide a much appreciated pause for breath before carrying on to the Abbey House. Of a very different architectural style to that of the palace, it was built in 1608 by Sir George's elder brother, Edward Bruce. It forms a fitting culmination to a tour of this most picturesque of Royal Burghs.

The Ross Fountain in Princes Street Gardens

The city from Corstorphine Hill

THE HOUSE OF THE BINNS

National Trust for Scotland Property

How to get there:
Signposted, off the A904, 15 miles west of Edinburgh

Car parking: Free

Open: House and grounds: daily except Fridays during May–September, 2.00–5.30
Grounds only: daily throughout year, 10.00–7.00

Price Guide: C
(Uniformed members of the Royal Scots Greys get in free)

Where to eat: Linlithgow, South Queensferry

Sheltered by centuries-old trees, The House of the Binns perches on the slopes of twin hills some 15 miles to the west of Edinburgh, and is still lived in by the Dalyell family whose ancestor bought the lands of The Binns – meaning 'hills' – and its accompanying manor way back in 1612. That ancester was Thomas Dalyell, an Edinburgh butter merchant who made his fortune during the ten years he spent in London at the court of James I after he became king of England.

Thomas spent the next 20 years enlarging and improving the house, a tradition which was carried on by his descendants to such an extent that some additions completely changed the face of the 1612 building, including moving the front door to the back, and vice versa.

By far the most prominent personality in the complex family tree was General Tam Dalyell, son of Thomas the butterman, about whom legend and fact are inextricably mingled, and whose relics still abound at The Binns today. Opting for a military career, Tam's exploits at one stage took him far from his native shores and into Russia, where he assisted in the reorganisation of the Russian army, was promoted to general, and made a noble of that country. But much of his career was spent in strife-torn seventeenth-century Scotland, and he is probably best remembered as the man who raised the Royal Regiment of Scots Dragoons, later known as the Royal Scots Greys, which held its first muster at The Binns.

The house holds an interesting collection of paintings, furniture, porcelain and china, silver and many objets d' art gathered together during more than three centuries. Particularly charming is the Blue Room, where the walls are covered with Chinese, Dutch and English willow-pattern ware.

The plaster ceilings in the first floor drawing room and the King's Bedroom are particularly fine. Dating from 1630, they were specially commissioned in the hope that Charles I would stay at The Binns during a tour of Scotland. Much to the disappointment of Thomas the butterman, the monarch declined.

An interesting insight into life below stairs is found in the kitchen, probably the former bakehouse, with its two ovens which were heated by burning wood inside, then raking out the fire before popping in the bread. Now flagged and equipped as it would have been in the seventeenth century, the kitchen with its spinning wheel, kettles, bed warmers, jelly pans and copper utensils make a fascinating cameo.

The Visitor Trail in the grounds is very pleasant, an avenue of limes leading one to the Binns Tower built by Sir James Dalyell in the 1800s at a cost of £29.10s, money which he had won in a bet! The Binns Tower provides extensive views over the Firth of Forth and the surrounding countryside, including the old shale bings which are a monument to the oil industry so vital to the area during the first half of the twentieth century.

The House of the Binns

DUNFERMLINE

Set in the ancient kingdom of Fife, and capital of Scotland for 36 short years nine centuries ago, is the historic town of Dunfermline, where the dusty shades of Scottish monarchs long since gone still linger among the stones of the abbey and the nearby palace ruins.

Resting-place of no fewer than 28 royals and six monarchs, not the least of whom was Robert the Bruce, today's abbey comprises two churches which in turn were built over two much earlier places of worship.

Dunfermline Abbey

What is generally regarded as the modern parish church, although it was dedicated in 1821, is easily identifiable by its square tower topped by the lattice-work of the lettering KING ROBERT THE BRUCE, one word to each of the four sides.

Built on the foundations of the choir of David I's Benedictine abbey of 1150, the church abutts on to the still-standing monastic nave which now serves as a vestibule. Excavations under the nave in 1916 produced two significant discoveries: the foundations of the small church built by Malcolm III for his Queen Margaret in about 1072, and the even earlier foundations of an undated Celtic church.

When the nave floor was replaced, five openings were left under iron grilles through which parts of these ancient remains can be seen, electrically lit by prior arrangement with the custodian.

The ruins of the Benedictine monastery founded about 1128 are across the site of the cloisters to the south of the nave. Much of the outer wall of the main building still stands, giving a good idea of its original three-storey layout.

The great pend or archway, which crosses Monastery Street and St Catherine's Wynd, linked the monastery with the kitchens and the guest wing, later to be enlarged and used as an occasional residence for royalty.

James VI of Scotland spent a considerable amount of time here, having the palace modernised and enlarged still further as a wedding gift for his Danish bride Anne, and it is said that he remained in residence, torn by grief, while his mother Mary Queen of Scots was being beheaded in London.

Little remains now of the palace, which can only be viewed from nearby paths, but the keen eye can spot the large window high in the west wing where Charles I was born.

While the abbey and palace must be regarded as the focal points of Dunfermline, it has other claims to fame.

Once a great linen weaving centre, it achieved worldwide fame in the nineteenth century with the development of damask, the name given to the figured patterns woven into linen. This was thanks to a somewhat underhand ruse on the part of a local weaver. Having heard of this new technique being practised in Edinburgh, he unobtrusively hung around the city workshops and managed to pick up enough about the secret processes to be able to rush home and start up in opposition!

Dunfermline Palace

ANDREW CARNEGIE – BENEFACTOR

One cannot walk far in Dunfermline without coming across reminders in some shape or form that it was here, amid the historical wealth of this ancient burgh, that the world's richest man was born in 1835.

Andrew Carnegie was the son of a local weaver, and where better to start tracing his meteoric rise to riches than in the simple little cottage that contained his birthplace, an attic room within sight of the abbey. It was a two-roomed, tiny place, with the father's hand-loom and workshop downstairs, and one room upstairs where the family lived.

Water and coal would have to be brought upstairs, and it is more than likely that Mrs Carnegie would have undertaken the task of filling the spools for her husband's loom, dropping them through a hole in the floor to the workroom below.

The little cottage has been arranged as it would have been in the young Carnegie's time, even to the two fixed beds along one wall, curtains being the only concession to privacy; rag rugs on the floor; plain but functional furniture; period cooking utensils; and the father's old loom downstairs.

The decline of the town's linen trade forced the impoverished family to emigrate to America when the boy was only 12. He started work in a Pittsburgh mill and, thanks to night classes and self-imposed reading, started up the ladder to success.

By 33, he was already a multi-millionaire, heading up a number of heavy industry companies which earned him the nickname King Steel. Such wealth he was not prepared to keep for himself or his family, preferring to take heed of the philanthropic side of his nature. So began a series of benefactions, trusts, and gifts, and by the end of his life in 1919 this self-made industrialist had given away nearly 70 million pounds. His first gift to Dunfermline was a library, one of nearly 3000 later endowed worldwide. Subsequent major gifts include the concert centre of the Carnegie Hall with its adjoining Music Institute.

When Andrew Carnegie was young the 76 acres of Pittencrief Park in the centre of Dunfermline was a paradise. He never forgot the joy it brought him, and in 1903, after he had made his millions in America, he bought the estate for £45,000 and presented the park, together with sufficient money in trust for its upkeep, to his home town so that it should provide 'sweetness and light for the toiling masses of Dunfermline'.

The toiling masses are joined these days by the thousands of visitors who come to enjoy the amenities of this rugged glen, wandering along its criss-crossing paths with their tantalising glimpses of the abbey and palace between the trees.

There are a number of entrances to the park, the main one being guarded by the massive gates which were erected in 1929 and named after Carnegie's wife, Louise, while a statue of the man himself stands in a nearby avenue. Once inside, there is much to see and do. The history lover will doubtless appreciate the remains of Malcolm III's Tower, stronghold of one of Scotland's earliest kings, and home of Malcolm and his bride of 1070, Margaret Atheling.

In the nearby ravine, one comes across an unexpected six-sided gazebo on the lines of a miniature bandstand, possibly erected as a viewpoint for the unusual double bridge spanning the river. This curious construction – a second and higher bridge surmounting an older one – is also found a few miles away at Rumbling Bridge, a hamlet which takes its name from the echoes of the waters as they tumble under the arch.

Standing stolidly in the middle of the park is Pittencrief House, a seventeenth-century fortified mansion which had a succession of owners before Carnegie handed the estate to the town. Now it is used mainly as a museum, which includes a costume gallery.

A formal garden has been laid out where once were the vegetable gardens and orchard for the mansion house, and nearby is a floral hall built in 1973 on the site of the previous conservatories. Two children's playgrounds and two paddling pools have been provided, with the additional attraction of the Animal Centre, aviaries, and a rabbit corner for the younger children. The park also has its own licensed restaurant and separate cafeteria.

Dunfermline, birthplace of Andrew Carnegie

HOPETOUN HOUSE

How to get there:
Car: Turn off A90 south of Forth Bridge on to A904 (Bo'ness Road) and follow Hopetoun signs
Bus: Special afternoon excursions 3 times weekly during summer through travel agents (or tel. Eastern Scottish Bus Company on 031-556 8464). Alternatively take regular bus to South Queensferry and walk, following Hopetoun signs

Car parking: Free, ample

Publications: In Reception Hall

Open: House and grounds: 11.00–5.30 daily, from end of April–September

Price Guide: C (house and grounds), B (grounds only)

Walled Garden Centre: Open all year 10.00–5.30

Where to eat: Restaurant or picnic areas

For impressive splendour on a grand scale, Hopetoun House has no equal among Scotland's stately mansions. But if you think of popping in to while away the odd half-hour – don't. The only possible way to appreciate the countless treasures from all corners of Europe amassed in its magnificent apartments, as well as the 100 acres of parkland, is to spend the best part of a day there.

A foretaste of what lies ahead comes as one rounds a bend in the drive to see the gracious frontage unveiled in all its awe-inspiring majesty, so huge that it is hard for the eye to comprehend at first glance.

The ancestral home of the Hope family, whose present head is the fourth Marquess of Linlithgow, the original house on the shores of the Firth of Forth near South Queensferry was designed for the first Earl of Hopetoun by Sir William Bruce, architect of Holyrood Palace. Work was completed in 1703, but after the Earl married, he decided to enlarge the house. In 1721 he engaged the services of William Adam, who produced what is now regarded as his greatest masterpiece. Much of the ornate interior decoration, completed by his son John in 1767, still survives in the main apartments, and so do many of the original hangings and furniture.

As it now stands, Hopetoun House is a merging of two distinct buildings in two different styles. The original square two-storey building, largely wood-panelled, remains as the nucleus at the west side of the main block, with its French windows – the first to be installed in Scotland – leading into the park.

When William Adam planned the enlargement, he virtually switched the house round by designing an east-facing frontage in classical Grecian style, flanked by curving colonnades linking the main structure with the north and south pavilions to complete a symmetrical facade. This new image was followed through by the creation of the elegant and lofty apartments, which contrast with the more sombre panelling favoured by Bruce.

It was, however, in the older part of the house where a hitherto unknown ceiling painting was discovered and revealed in 1985, a find all the more remarkable because it has been dated back to the time of the original 1703 building. Its restoration necessitated the removal of seven coats of white paint, but why it should have been painted over in the first place remains a mystery.

The ceiling is over the original Bruce stairwell and comprises a series of allegorical scenes which cover the entire inner surface of the cupola. It is the only major ceiling painting of the Baroque period in any Scottish stately home, and in fact this type of decoration on such a scale is uncommon even in England.

It was obviously designed to link in with other canvas paintings of the same period once built into the staircase panelling. Called the 'Apotheosis of The Hope Family', angels and cherubs support the Hope crest and coat-of-arms, while scenes from The Labours of Hercules and The Story of Troy complete the ceiling. The painter is not identified but, since the painting is done straight on to the plaster of the cupola, he is believed to have been a Scottish decorative painter of the 1700–1710 period.

During a tour of Hopetoun House, over which you can linger as long as you like, with knowledgeable guides in most rooms to answer any little queries not covered by the literature, it is easy to be sidetracked by fascinating detail. In the Bruce Bedroom is the four-poster in which Queen Victoria slept, and which still wears its original crimson drapes. One wonders if Her Majesty would have been amused to know that her bed was brought by sea from London to Leith in D.I.Y. sections, transferred to horse and cart for the journey to Hopetoun, and then assembled by estate workers.

Four-posters were, of course, the order of the day, and many are to be found in the other bedrooms whose walls are hung with exquisite seventeenth-century tapestries brought from Antwerp. The little corner-wise fireplaces in these bedrooms, each with its cast-iron fire basket, were individually wrought by a local smith. They are as charming in their own way as the heavy sculpted marble chimney-pieces of the main apartments downstairs.

Also made locally were the wrought-iron balusters of the service stairs which run from the basement quarters to the servants' attic bedrooms. The handrail is high by modern standards, but then how many of us need to consider the safety of exceptionally tall footmen?

The Serving Room is a reminder of the days when food had to be trundled through the vast kitchen downstairs to the dumb waiter for its journey upstairs, then kept warm in a hot cupboard before being presented by the butler and his staff to the neighbouring dining room.

On display in the servery are the brass bells with which the household summoned its servants. The gleaming bells may appear to be a haphazard collection of shapes, sizes, and ringing tones, but as most servants of 200 years ago were illiterate, they had to rely on sight and sound to identify who was wanted where and by whom!

A bell of another sort is in the museum high up in the house. Made in Copenhagen in 1781, the bell is said to have been taken from a Danish man o' war captured by Nelson at the Battle of Copenhagen in 1805, and hung for many years in nearby Abercorn Church. The museum houses displays of family papers, china, costume, and other relics of a bygone age, including an 1870 boneshaker bicycle.

The stable block, well-disguised in the north wing of the new mansion, should not be overlooked. Surmounted by its own clocktower and providing stabling for 32 horses, with granaries and grooms' accommodation on the upper floor, it holds an interesting exhibition showing the role played by horse and man in this part of Scotland since the 1700s.

Old pages from accounting ledgers make fascinating reading. Today's head groom would be hard put to be able to buy six yards of girthing for 1/6d; a whip for 10d; or a cart saddle for 5/-. Close by, but hidden from the view of the gentry, is a self-contained complex of coach houses, tack rooms, smiddy and joiners' shop.

The nature trail through the beautifully kept parkland starts near the stables, and the visitor also has the opportunity of seeing a flock of rare four-horned St Kilda sheep and the herds of red and fallow deer before going on to explore the walled garden or gift shop.

In 1974 the Hope family established a charitable trust which now owns and preserves the house and estate for the benefit of the public, but the family still keep their roots at Hopetoun as tenants in part of the ancestral home.

DALMENY HOUSE

How to get there:
Car: A90 towards Forth Road Bridge. Then B924 following Dalmeny signs
Bus: From St Andrew Square to Chapel Gate, 1 mile from Dalmeny House

Car parking: Free, ample

Open: Sunday–Thursday, May–September, 2.00–5.30

Price Guide: C

Where to eat:
Home-made teas available

No picnics or dogs

The Rosebery estates in the east of Scotland are vast, and at the hub of them stands Dalmeny House, the sturdy Tudor Gothic mansion which has been the seat of the Primrose family since it was built in 1815, and which is very much home to the seventh Earl of Rosebery and his Countess.

Built on lands bought by the first Earl in 1662, the present house, with its abundance of tall ornamental chimneys and towers which are more reminiscent of Norfolk than the plainer architecture of lowland Scotland, replaced the original seat at neighbouring Barnbougle Castle. This was a thirteenth-century pile right on the seashore between Cramond and South Queensferry. Never a particularly comfortable place to live in, apparently the decision to rebuild further inland was clinched when a huge wave crashed through the dining-room window one stormy afternoon.

It is fortunate that such a mishap is unlikely to occur at Dalmeny, for it is here that the precious Mentmore Collection of eighteenth-century French furniture, porcelain, and other works of art have come to rest.

Many people will remember the furore surrounding the Mentmore sale in 1977 when the fabulous Rothschild collection came under the auctioneer's hammer. Related to the Rothschilds by marriage, Lord and Lady Rosebery had the foresight to select and preserve the finest pieces of their heritage to bring home to Scotland, before the sale irrevocably dispersed the treasures of Mentmore Towers to all parts of the globe.

In complete contrast to the graceful elegance of the Regency drawing-room is the French collection of a very different sort in the Napoleon Room. The fifth Earl, fascinated by the history of the emperor, brought to Dalmeny furniture and other memorabilia which traced Napleon's life from the height of his career to the ignominy of his exile.

Portraits of Napoleon, and of course the Empress Josephine, hang on the walls and gaze down, not only on the splendid furniture used by him when at the pinnacle of power, but also the simple desk and chairs of later years.

Ironically, this room also houses the red leather campaign chair used by his arch-foe, the Duke of Wellington, when he finally defeated Napoleon at the Battle of Waterloo.

Leaving for a while the portraits by Gainsborough, Reynolds and other contemporary artists, the Goya tapestries, the delicately-patterned carpets, and the sixteenth-century Scottish furniture brought from Barnbougle Castle, the visitor is jolted much nearer to the present day by the comfortable quiet of the late Lord Rosebery's study-cum-sitting-room.

Statue of *King Tom*

A life-long sportsman and one-time Surrey cricket captain, he was particularly noted for his associations with the turf. All this is reflected in the innumerable racing and hunting prints and photographs, the familiar racing colours of pink and primrose, and mementoes of the Derby winners and other champions bred at Mentmore stud.

Indeed, much of Dalmeny's charm lies in its lived-in atmosphere. The family may retire upstairs to their own apartments when visitors roam the premises, but the library – holding the fifth Earl's book collection is obviously still used as a sitting-room when the house is closed to the public. The dining-room is not just a showpiece either.

Stately mansion it may be, but thanks to the way in which Lord and Lady Rosebery have chosen to share their many treasures within the community where they play such an active part, Dalmeny still remains very much a home.

Napoleon Room

LAURISTON CASTLE

Lauriston Castle

How to get there:
Car: Take A90 north, turn off at Quality Street junction 3 miles from Princes Street
Well signposted
Bus: No. 41 from Princes Street

Car parking: Free

Open: Castle: April–October daily, except Friday, 11.00–1.00, 2.00–5.00
November–March weekends only, 2.00–4.00. Grounds open all year

Price Guide: B (castle), grounds free

Handicapped: Grounds suitable

Publications: From custodian

Where to eat: Nearby tea-room at former Lauriston Home Farm; or in Davidsons' Mains

Nearby Attraction: Cramond village

The fascination of Lauriston Castle lies not so much in the age of the building, but in the discovery that its furnishings are exactly the same as they were more than 60 years ago, when the last occupants bequeathed their home to the nation in the hope that it would serve to educate public taste.

Public taste has changed considerably since then, but it is an education in itself to see how the Edwardian mind saw fit to squash as much furniture as possible into the available space, including the bathroom, cover the walls with as many irrelevant prints and pictures as possible, fill a library with a hotch-potch of tomes, and perch ornaments on almost every flat surface.

The lands of Lauriston can be traced back to 1290 when it was apparently a farm belonging to the Crown, but the inevitable alterations and additions made by a remarkably long list of successive owners obviously presented a professional challenge to Edinburgh cabinet-maker and restorer William Robert Reid, who bought the castle in 1907.

Interior of the Castle

When the Reids moved in, the building was empty and in poor repair. Their aim was to transform it into an elegant home, a showpiece of fine furniture and objets d'art, and since they could well be described as cultural magpies, they succeeded almost to the point of suffocation!

So much has been said about the development over the centuries of this or that building that it makes a pleasant change to come across a place bearing the imprint of people closer to our own era, who wanted to carry on a tradition with the old mansion but incorporate into it the more personal atmosphere of possessions which go to make a home. That is what the Reids tried to do. Their ideas may seem quaint to us, but at Lauriston we are looking at something which is not too far hidden in the depths – something of which many of us can say 'that was Grannie'.

Much of Mr Reid's business involved the fitting out of ships' cabins and Pullman rail coaches. The wall-to-wall carpeting, quite an innovation for that period, bears a strong resemblance to the patterned carpeting found in older railway carriages, and the exceptionally deep bath with shower looks not unlike a ship's bath – it *is* a ship's bath!

Dominating the sitting room is an enormous cabinet displaying a collection of Derbyshire Blue John ware of all shapes and sizes. Blue John is a mineral mined near Castleton, and one wonders what prompted the Reids to assiduously gather together craftwork so very un-Scottish.

The Crossley wool mosaics which hang in the entrance hall are a remarkable example of an advertising technique long since overtaken by paper posters, and it is fortunate that Mr Reid saw fit to preserve these delightful wool pictures. The same could be said for the framed prints and books in the library. Bought in job lots for a song, they were recently catalogued for Edinburgh District Council, who administer the property, and found to be more valuable than expected.

Lauriston is not only a showplace for period pieces and the reproduction furniture made by Mr Reid. There are disguised or fake doorways; Dutch stained glass window panels; 300-year-old Flemish tapestries; objets d'art from all over Europe; and tucked away in the panelling of a window embrasure, the entrance to a spiral stair leading up to a secret room.

The oldest part of the building is the turreted tower house, built in about 1590. This was extended to become the gracious country mansion of today in the 1800s, so one has the contrasting architecture of the south-facing tower house and the elegance of the Jacobean-style north facade. From here, there are superb views over the great expanse of lawn to the Forth, while the parkland in which the castle stands provides delightful walks.

Bo'ness and Kinneil Railway

419 steaming towards Kinneil Halt

The buildings are an attraction in themselves in that they are genuine antiques gathered by the Society as British Rail gradually closed down small stations after 1956. Typical of such small stations, with its canopy of elaborate woodwork and miniature ticket window in the booking hall, is the main station building. This came from Wormit, in Fife, where in exchange for £300 paid to British Rail in 1980, members found themselves facing the task of breaking the century-old brick and timber structure down into manageable pieces and loading them on to road transport for the move to Bo'ness.

There was a heartfelt sigh of relief when, on arrival, the stationmaster's office more or less fitted the brick base prepared for it. Over the next few months, the rest was lovingly re-assembled, repaired, and in fact virtually rebuilt to produce an exact replica.

At the western end of the platform is the train shed, formerly at Haymarket station in Edinburgh. This dates from the opening in 1842 of Scotland's first main line railway linking Glasgow and Edinburgh; Haymarket was the original eastern terminus. The ironwork of the shed is a fine example of the elaborate ornamentation so beloved by the Victorians.

The footbridge which gives access to the old dockside and walk-about area was constructed at Inverness for the Highland Railway, and came from Murthly, north of Perth. Watching overall is the timber signal box which once stood at Garnqueen South Junction near Coatbridge, on the old Caledonian Railway.

At the goods shed, the way in which freight traffic was handled is shown. The cast-iron wagon turntable – from Leith – allowed single wagons to be manoeuvred into convenient positions for loading and unloading. Since this prevented the use of locomotives for shunting, horses had to be employed. The pillar crane, which is hand-operated, will lift two tons.

The track itself once formed part of the freight line from Kinneil Colliery, and was bought in 1978 for the SRPS, who re-laid it to form the 1¼-mile run between Bo'ness and Kinneil. The Society has plans for the eventual extension of the track.

The engines are many and varied: from a small industrial type built in Newcastle in 1926 to the almost outsize No. 1313 from the Swedish State Railways, built in 1917. But the one which takes pride of place is No. 419, the last remaining engine from the Caledonian Railway in regular service.

Likewise, the coaches come from a wide variety of sources. The oldest was built in 1919 for the North British Railway, and was originally an invalid saloon which could be hired by those whose pockets were deep enough, and attached to whichever train they wished in the region. Today, it is generally used as the station buffet.

Nostalgia for the grown-ups; a whole new experience for the rising generation. That could aptly describe the effect of any visit to the Bo'ness & Kinneil Railway in West Lothian, where the enthusiastic members of the Scottish Railway Preservation Society painstakingly labour in their spare time to bring back to life the sights and smells of the age of the steam train.

Anyone approaching Bo'ness station today may well be forgiven for not realising that, in 1978, the site was no more than a stretch of derelict grassy scrubland. Since then, the atmosphere of a Scottish country station has been built up, and will continue to be improved and enlarged upon for years to come.

Of much more recent vintage is a 1940s coach from the London & North Eastern Railway, painted in the 'simulated teak' then used to make the steel coaches blend in with the genuine teak vehicles of an earlier era. In complete contrast is the set of four wooden-bodied coaches and luggage van from Norway which form a complete 'Scandinavian Vintage Train' when coupled to the Swedish engine.

All this rolling stock does not just sit looking pretty at Bo'ness – it is there to be used and enjoyed, even though the round trip only lasts about 20 minutes.

Every weekend during the summer, a modest train of two or three interesting old coaches and a steam engine can be caught at Bo'ness station. Leaving the platform the track runs alongside the once-busy harbour, passing the former Customs House which now does duty as commercial premises. Across the Forth can be seen the already-restored village of Culross, and the more distant mountains of Perthshire.

The train then passes the original Bo'ness passenger station, which was closed in 1956 and of which there is very little trace, before arriving at Kinneil. Here, the engine has to be uncoupled to allow it to be moved to the other end of the train for the return trip.

No doubt the curious are still wondering how the name Bo'ness came about. In fact it is generally accepted to be a contraction of the tongue-twisting Borrowstoun-ness. And for those interested in the macabre, a number of witches and wizards were tried and burned there in 1679!

KINNEIL HOUSE

It was appropriate that the Scottish Railway Preservation Society decided to link Bo'ness and Kinneil in their ambitious project, for it was in an outhouse at Kinneil House that James Watt perfected his steam engine in 1765.

No doubt he would have been sad to see Kinneil House (once called Kinneil Palace) as we see it today. Even in Watt's time, much of the original mid-sixteenth-century keep had already disappeared, demolished in a local feud, although one wall overhanging the ravine of the Gil Burn still forms part of the now roofless central block. Over the next 100 years or so the owners added extensions here and there, and inevitably, as time went by, some of these deteriorated until the building was taken in hand comparatively recently.

Despite the partial restoration which has been done, Kinneil House still shows a plain, uninspiring exterior, so visitors receive a pleasant surprise on going indoors. Restoration work in two rooms on the first floor revealed, hidden behind the plastering, mural tempera paintings which are now regarded as amongst the finest in Scotland. One room, the Parable Room, has six episodes from the parable of the Good Samaritan, with life-size figures painted against a scenic background. The adjoining Arbour Room shows other Biblical subjects below a frieze of birds and animals.

Hand Operated Crane

LINLITHGOW

Linlithgow, situated half-way between Edinburgh and Glasgow, is a bustling county town whose buildings are a pleasing mixture of ancient and modern. Boutiques and shoe shops rub shoulders with quaint pubs and tea rooms, and even the chain stores seem to keep a low profile. Above them all, the scene is dominated by the historic Palace of Linlithgow, built on the banks of the loch, and the birthplace of Mary, Queen of Scots, in 1542.

The town began as a cluster of medieval huts huddled near a fortified royal manor house, built by David I in the twelfth century on the site later used for the palace. Gradually the town developed eastwards and westwards along the line of today's High Street.

The palace itself was started in 1425 by James I of Scotland, and subsequent monarchs carried out the inevitable additions and improvements. On the first floor is the great hall, or Lyon Chamber, occupying the whole of one side of the palace, and it was here that the Scottish parliament met in 1585.

Several Scottish kings lived at the palace, and James V in particular left his mark. The fountain in the courtyard was commissioned by him in 1530, and the palace gateway bears panels representing his Orders of Knighthood – the Golden Fleece, St Michael, the Garter and the Thistle.

There were fewer royal visits after the union of Scotland with England, and the palace gradually declined in importance. Finally in 1746 soldiers billeted there inadvertently started a fire which destroyed much of the building, leaving the partial ruin we see today. Nearby is the pre-Reformation Church of St Michael's, easily distinguishable by its contemporary-style spire which was the cause of many a raised eyebrow, not to say heated controversy.

During the mid-1700s Linlithgow had a thriving linen-making industry, and it was a common sight to see the banks of the loch draped with yards of linen laid out to bleach. This trade has disappeared now, as have the damask, muslin and carpet manufacturers.

The town was perhaps better known for tanning, shoemaking and gluemaking, the first two reputedly introduced by Cromwell's men during their occupation in the mid-1600s. Only traces of the buildings and machinery now remain to mark the 17 tanneries, 12 skinneries, and 18 currying (leather dressing) establishments which once played such an important part in the town's economy.

Behind the palace is Linlithgow Loch, one of the few remaining undrained natural lochs in West Lothian, and with a wealth of wildlife to be seen during the hour or so it takes to walk round the 100-acre stretch of water. Swans have been known to nest there for centuries, but legend has it that when Cromwell's troops entered the town, the swans promptly left, returning only when Charles II was restored to the throne.

The swans could have had good reason for leaving, though, as in Cromwell's time the waters of the loch were used in the leather tanning trade. His troops are supposed to have instructed local craftsmen in the art of steeping raw hides in water containing oak bark to provide the tannin.

Be that as it may, the swans and ducks now swim serenely on the loch, undisturbed except by passing walkers and the occasional angler in his rowing boat. Also left undisturbed are the inhabitants of the sheltered bird sanctuaries, from which walkers are excluded, but the slight detours involved in no way detract from the superb views over loch, palace and town.

One way and another, water has played a considerable part in Linlithgow's social and economic history. Part of the Edinburgh and Glasgow Union Canal still winds its way through the town on its now curtailed route. Linlithgow Basin was a busy stopping place for canal traffic with tolls being charged on cargoes passing through. Coal mined locally was the most important cargo, but the canal also carried merchandise and other goods westward from Edinburgh.

Commercial traffic died out in 1933, and 1965 saw the closure of the canal as a thoroughfare. Ten years later the Linlithgow Union Canal Society was formed, opening its museum at The Basin near the centre of the town in 1977. Here can be seen visual displays of the construction, decline and restoration of the canal. The society owns several boats. The best-known is *Victoria*, a replica of a Victorian packet boat, which carries visitors for a short cruise along a stretch of the canal during summer

weekend afternoons, and longer evening cruises on Fridays.

Re-enacting the storming of the Palace by Cromwell's Roundheads, at the annual Linlithgow pageant.

CAIRNPAPPLE

One day an airman flying towards Edinburgh glanced curiously at the high ground below him. He was puzzled. There appeared to be a symmetrical arrangement of humps and indentations on top of the hill he was passing over between Bathgate and Linlithgow, north of the Edinburgh–Glasgow road.

That was in 1936. The war intervened, and it was not until 1947 that Edinburgh University began excavating the site. The results after a two-year dig were astounding – the pilot had spotted what turned out to be a Neolithic sanctuary dating back to 3000 BC, the earliest known archaeological relic in Scotland.

Before excavations began, the site from ground level looked to be merely a cairn-topped hill. As work progressed, archaeologists discovered that here they had a complex structure which spelled out clearly five different phases of prehistoric man's burial rituals.

It appears that man has always had a desire to extend and improve on earlier constructions, for as layer after layer was uncovered it was possible to trace the history of the Cairnpapple site from its beginnings as a burial mound in the Stone Age through its later phases: a temple in the early Bronze Age, a cairn in the later Bronze Age, and a burial ground in the Iron Age.

Earthworks, stone circles, ditches, graves, and great stone kerbs had all been added or re-located during the centuries until it lost its religious importance and fell into disuse around the first century AD, becoming hidden under a camouflage of clay, silted earth and grass.

One has to be sound in wind and limb to tackle the stiff climb from the small car park area up to the summit of the thousand-foot high Cairnpapple Hill, but the effort is well worthwhile.

The Bronze Age cairn was reconstructed with a concrete dome after the excavations, and an iron ladder through an opening in the top leads down to the interior. Here can be seen the stones of two of the earliest graves or burial cists, re-sited as they would have been placed nearly 5000 years ago. Most of the many artefacts found, including food vessels and pottery urns or beakers – from which the prehistoric builders take the name Beaker People – are now in the Huntly House Museum in Edinburgh.

Beaker People were peace-loving, and the choice of this hilltop as a religious place was possibly governed, not by defensive considerations, but by the extensive all-round views it provides, with the Bass Rock visible 40 miles to the east, and the Isle of Arran to the west.

On nearby hills are a number of single standing stones, and it is believed that these cairns were used as beacons to guide travellers to and from the sanctuary. It is known that the Beaker People bartered their animal skins and pottery in exchange for stone axeheads which had been quarried as far away as Westmorland and North Wales.

Cairnpapple was not the only treasure hidden in the Bathgate hills. On another slope can be found the grass-covered shallow terraces where silver was once mined. The silver ore was discovered in the early 1600s, and a lump was sent to James VI in London. As Parliament seemed unable to realise just how much money a king needed to indulge his tastes, James hailed it as the answer to his financial prayers and promptly nationalised the mine. Unfortunately the venture was short-lived, but the terraces remain as a reminder that one never knows what one may find in 'them thar hills'.

LIVINGSTON MILL FARM

One of the few working mills in the east of Scotland is at Livingston Mill Farm, where a voluntary community organisation has spent a number of years restoring and rebuilding the eighteenth-century farm and mill buildings to create a small operational unit and countryside museum.

One of the farm's friendly goats

The farm, bounded on one side by the river Almond which provides the water power, covers about 6½ acres to the west of old Livingston village – itself a conservation area, and in no way to be confused with the enormous concrete jungle of Livingston new town a few miles away.

Built in 1770, the mill and kiln was a working unit right up to the mid-1900s, and its life was further extended by the efforts of local people who restored the waterwheel as a replica of the original. Further major restoration work, now features the 42-paddle waterwheel, 16 feet in diameter and four feet wide; the huge mill-stones; and the reconstructed grain-drying kiln which was heated by a great furnace in its working days, and capable of processing eight bags of grain at a time spread over the drying floor.

Much of the machinery for winnowing, threshing, chaff cutting and animal feed processing has been restored in order to provide working exhibits, and former loose boxes have been converted into an engine house to accommodate a steam engine and boiler.

The greater part of the farm steading includes three large stables, a traditional byre, and three smaller animal enclosures, all displaying farm tools, implements and wagons from the last century. Part of the steading is also used to show and encourage the proper management of household pets. The farmyard itself includes housing for the hens and rabbits, as well as providing a children's play area, and the mill pond is a natural habitat for ducks, geese and other waterfowl, which can also be seen on the nature trail which encompasses the farm, weir, mill lade and river bank.

Running loose in the paddock for much of the day is the farm's collection of docile livestock. A firm favourite is Ben, the gentle giant of a Clydesdale horse which once pulled a milk float in Edinburgh, and at the other end of the scale is Duncan, the Shetland pony. There are also sheep, calves, and some very inquisitive and friendly goats!

The main aim of the project is to provide an educational facility, and the buildings incorporate a meeting/study room seating 30 to 40 people which is equipped with audio-visual services. The Farm Kitchen Cafe provides refreshments, and there is also a tourist centre, with adequate car parking and access for the handicapped.

Although primarily geared towards weekday school parties, Livingston Mill Farm is open to other visitors at weekends during the summer months. Further information may be obtained by telephoning Livingston 414957.

Ben, a Clydesdale horse

THE ROYAL HIGHLAND SHOW

The Royal Highland Show is the largest single event in Scotland, attracting around 150,000 visitors during its four-day run. Held every mid-June at Ingliston, near Edinburgh, it draws its crowds from town and country and overseas, as individuals or as family groups. In those four days, the 110 acres of the showground take on a holiday atmosphere, promoted from the start by Scottish Brewers' Sunday, essentially a family occasion with a wide range of entertainments varying from year to year.

The main theme, of course, is agriculture, the country's main industry, and around 4000 head of livestock are usually entered for the show, competing for prize money and trophies worth £350,000. More than 700 trade stands cover every type of farm machinery and allied equipment.

The tented flower show, the largest of its kind in Scotland, houses magnificent displays arranged by local authorities and organisations as well as overseas exhibits. Fashion shows and cookery demonstrations are held daily, and handiwork produced by the Scottish Women's Rural Institutes give a fine insight into traditional country crafts. Top riders travel to Ingliston to compete in the various show jumping classes; from nearer home, farriers and shepherds race against the clock in the horse-shoeing or sheep-shearing competitions.

In 1979 the Exhibition Hall was opened on the showground. This is used throughout the year for various events, and during the show it provides a giant shopping arcade selling a wide variety of goods from china to shoes, clothing to ironmongery. Nearby is the Food Fair offering an abundance of produce from abroad as well as a comprehensive range of Scottish foods.

The organisers of what is referred to locally as simply 'the Highland', are the Royal Highland and Agricultural Society of Scotland, whose founders held their first general meeting in the Royal Exchange Coffee House in Edinburgh on March 12, 1784. Until 1958, the event moved around the country to the main agricultural centres, but in that year the site at Ingliston was acquired, and two years later the first show was held at its now permanent home. The past 200 years have seen the development of many ideas sponsored by the Society, not the least of which is an annual attraction providing as much interest for the townsman as for the countryman.

Shaggy Highland cattle show off their offspring

CORSTORPHINE

Corstorphine, the pronunciation of which baffles most outsiders, is a city village which doggedly clings to its community spirit and historical associations despite the onslaught of suburban development.

Certainly it has been an inhabited area for centuries, as evidence of a Roman stone embankment was found at the western end of what had been Corstorphine Loch during local building excavations a few years ago. Here there was a Roman fort, and Corstorphine itself is thought to have been near the intersection of two Roman roads.

The main thoroughfare today is St Johns Road, with its apparently permanent traffic bottleneck, but from its south side Kirk Loan leads to the centre of the old village and the church built in 1429 by Sir John Forrester. Much of the original fabric of this compact building still remains, with heavy buttresses, perpendicular tracery, a squat tower with stone spire, and the most striking feature of all, a roof of great stone slabs. Inside are the tombs and effigies of the Forresters. High in the wall can be seen the niche where a lamp was kept lit at night to guide travellers safely over the marshes and loch which split Corstorphine and Edinburgh. For providing the light for the lantern, the schoolmaster at

Corstorphine Dovecot

Corstorphine was rewarded with the gift of an acre of land by Lord George Forrester.

The Forrester family had been connected with the village for centuries, having acquired the lands in 1376. It was they who lived in the grandeur of Corstorphine Castle, now completely disappeared except for the large round dovecot tapering towards a stone-slabbed roof, with more than 1000 nesting holes.

Almost hanging over the dovecot is the 400-year-old sycamore tree, thought to be the only survivor of what could have been a tree-lined avenue leading to the castle. Trees are often traditional lovers' trysting-places, and this tree is no exception. Legend has it that Christian Nimmo, wife of an Edinburgh merchant, was in love with James, Laird of Forrester. Meeting under the tree one winter's night, they quarrelled about his drinking habits, and in her anger, Christian pulled his sword and killed him, an act for which she was beheaded in 1698. Known as the White Lady of Corstorphine, her ghostly figure still wanders near the sycamore carrying her lover's bloodied sword.

In the mid-1700s, the village suddenly found itself a tourist attraction, thanks to the Physic Well further along the High Street. Its medicinal properties became so well-known that by 1749, a coach ran between Edinburgh and Corstorphine eight or nine times a day, and four times on a Sunday (at a fare of sixpence!) so that visitors could take the waters. However, this early tourist trade ended when a nearby ditch, known inelegantly as the Stank Burn, was deepened and the Physic Well lost its properties.

Not too far away from the Physic Well was the site of Our Lady's Well which was one of many supplying the village's water needs until the 1880s. Perhaps it is appropriate that the area known as Ladywell now includes the local medical centre!

Edinburgh from
Corstorphine Hill

EDINBURGH TAPESTRY COMPANY

In a modest house in a secluded Corstorphine street, only distinguishable from its residential neighbours by the small nameplate on the garden gate and the old dovecot from which it takes its name, the Edinburgh Tapestry Company is a unique blend of the traditional, contemporary and futuristic. This unpretentious studio is the only tapestry workshop in Scotland, and with more of its production going to overseas buyers than remaining in this country, it is now recognised as a world leader in the craft.

The modern revival of interest in tapestry was largely due to the influence of the artist William Morris, the pioneer behind the famous tapestry firm which operated from Merton Abbey near Wimbledon. At the turn of the century, inspired by the work being done there, the third Marquess of Bute decided to establish a weaving workshop in Scotland. He died before his plan was realised, but his son carried on with the project and the Dovecot Studio enterprise was founded in 1912.

Work came to an abrupt halt when the weavers enlisted at the outbreak of the Second World War, and an interesting relic of this period remains at the studio: an unfinished tapestry, the 'Raising of The Standard', still on its loom as it was left in 1939 – its weavers killed in action on the battlefields of France.

During the years since the studio re-opened in 1946, the style of work has veered away from the historic and landscape tradition, and has entered a whole new artistic phase with the production of abstract works. In December 1984 the studio received its largest-ever commission, worth £180,000, comprising eleven tapestries, each more than seven feet square, designed to enhance the world headquarters of a soft drinks company in New York.

The designs may be modernistic, and materials updated to include synthetics, but the skills of the six weavers are unaltered for the very good reason that there is no machine yet invented capable of doing their intricate handcraft.

Before any tapestry is started the studio staff discuss materials and techniques to be used, the correct blend or mix of colours required, and prepare sample pieces from the hundreds of shades and fibres available. Once the upright warps have been attached to the rollers, full-size photographic enlargements of the artist's basic design are placed behind the vertical strands and the outline is inked-on, providing guidelines for shapes and colours.

As work on a tapestry progresses, the weavers have to rely on their own expertise to make any minor adjustments as they twist the bobbins between the warps, the pattern gradually emerging as horizontal weft builds up inch by inch. With the large tapestries, it is usual for three weavers to work side by side, and as the maximum working height is reached, the tapestry is wound on to the bottom roller – a frustrating necessity, as the artist may lose sight of most of his design for the best part of a year or more!

Tapestry weaving at Corstorphine

EDINBURGH ZOO

How to get there:
Car: Approx. 2½ miles
from Princes Street on
Glasgow road
Bus: Most west-bound
city services from Princes
Street

Car parking: 50p per
vehicle

Open: Every day
throughout the year
Summer 9.00–6.00;
winter 9.00–5.00 (or
dusk)
Sundays from 9.30

Price Guide: D

Handicapped: Partially
suitable

Publications: At
entrance complex and
shop

Where to eat: Licensed
restaurant; picnic room
Ices, drinks, sweets at
various kiosks

It was the dogged determination of one man, encouraged by only a handful of friends, which gave Edinburgh its famous zoo, the largest and oldest animal park in Scotland, and without doubt the city's major year-round attraction. So accustomed are residents and visitors to its presence that one tends to forget that someone founded it, that it did not just happen.

Thomas Gillespie, whose own back garden bore a strong resemblance to a miniature zoo, began his efforts to establish a national zoological park for Scotland as far back as 1908. It was months before he was able to gather round him sufficient interested people to form the Zoological Society of Scotland – and even then, a passer-by had to be pulled off the street into one meeting to make up the required quorum of ten!

A suitable site at a suitable price for the Society's meagre funds was the next priority. When the estate of Corstorphine Hill House was offered to the society in 1912 the opportunity was too good to miss. The site could not have been bettered. Covering nearly 80 acres on the southern slopes of Corstorphine Hill, protected from the cold northerly winds by its summit height of 550 feet above sea level and well clad with timber, the estate came complete with the house, gardens and outbuildings.

With Mr Gillespie as its first director, the society's plan for the park was to follow the example set by Carl Hagenbeck at the relatively new and highly successful Hamburg Zoo. The animals were to be exhibited in the most natural surroundings possible, with main enclosures bounded by rock cliffs and hidden ditches instead of the old concept of iron bars.

The official opening of Edinburgh Zoo was fixed for July 1913, and within a matter of weeks following the purchase of the estate the roads and paths were laid, and existing small quarries on the hill were adapted for outside enclosures such as the polar bear pool and lions' den. Open-air cages and aviaries were prepared, and ponds made ready for their new tenants; just as importantly, alterations had to be made to the house to provide a restaurant and other facilities for visitors.

A zoo's not a zoo without its resident population, and the very first purchase made by Mr Gillespie was a fledgling gannet, blown on to the West Pier at Leith, and which he was able to buy for the large sum of eighteen pence. Next to come on this unusual shopping list were two young brown bears and a polar bear which were acquired from the old Marine Gardens at Portobello.

Although some animals had already been gifted to the society, as opening day drew nearer they were still so thin on the ground that at one stage Mr Gillespie even contemplated the possibility of some sort of hire-purchase arrangement with Hamburg. Fortunately, the situation was saved by the loan of a private collection from Maidstone. The animals were brought north to the local railway station in two large railway parcel vans, and transferred to lorries for the final lap to the zoo, followed sedately by two camels on foot. It is unlikely that local residents will ever see such a parade again, barring the coming of a second Ark!

During the next months, the zoo's own collection increased at an impressive rate. New additions included a pair of lions from the Royal Zoological Society of Ireland; a much-prized baby elephant from the Maharajah of Mysore; and a considerable cross-section of creatures great and small, not the least important being six penguins – the ancestors of those who today make up the largest penguin colony in Europe.

With the outbreak of World War II, preparations were made to cope with both animals and visitors during air raids. Indeed, the old Carnegie Aquarium was used on occasions as a shelter during alarms. The keepers were armed, for theirs was a double task: not only might they have had to deal with any enemy dropping by, but they also had the necessary but distasteful job of destroying any of their charges should the animals be injured or let loose from their enclosures. Fortunately, the keepers were not called upon for either duty.

Two high-explosive bombs did, in fact, fall on the park one night in November 1940, and since the damage centred round the aviaries, ape house and reptile house, all of which had their glass shattered, it is fair to assume the bombers thought they were aiming at the glinting windows of some factory.

Trixie the Sea lion greets a young visitor

Proud Siberian tiger guards her three cubs

More welcome visitors received at the zoo over the years have been members of the Royal Family, and heads of overseas states with their entourages. What must have been the society's proudest moment, and a fitting tribute to the work put in by Mr Gillespie from those early beginnings, was when King George VI granted the coveted prefix which made it the Royal Zoological Society of Scotland.

So that was the past – what of the present? There are now more than 1000 animals on display; many are endangered species, threatened with extinction by the destruction of their natural habitat. Breeding groups in captivity are helping the survival of these animals, and with co-operation between zoos increasing worldwide, more and more endangered animals are being loaned for breeding purposes, so reducing the drain on wild populations.

For example, July 1985 saw the arrival of the first-ever gorillas in Scotland, Sam Sam from Rotterdam Zoo, and Naomi from Bristol Zoo, in one of the many exchange programmes operating between zoos internationally. In the same year, a similar exchange brought together two Siberian tigers, Ivan from Minnesota Zoo and Paula from Marwell Zoo in England – apparently an acceptable situation as they quickly started producing offspring! Siberian tigers are very much an endangered species, as it is estimated there are only about 300 left in the wild. In 1986, a pair of snow leopards joined the expanding family of big cats.

High up on the hill, a large undulating area with trees and grassy knolls has been christened the African Plains, and here can be found free-running herds of three animals from that continent – zebra, lechwe antelopes, and the scimitar-horned oryx. In 1987, a small group of oryx from Edinburgh were re-introduced to the wild in a Tunisian game reserve, thus helping to perpetuate the species in something like its natural environment.

Always a great attraction are the animal feeding sessions, particularly the sea lions and penguins. During the summer months visitors are treated to the sight of the great colony of penguins taking its keepers for an afternoon walk across the grassy area in front of their enclosure.

As well as the displays in the entrance complex to encourage public awareness and interest in the importance of wildlife conservation, the society also operates a scheme whereby individuals and organisations are invited to assist the zoo by adopting one or more of the inmates, and contributing towards its upkeep – from the majestic lion to the humblest toad. In this way we can all help to preserve the rich wildlife heritage that inspired the zoo's founder, Thomas Gillespie, all those years ago.

EDINBURGH CASTLE

Open:
October–March:
Mon–Sat: 9.30
am–4.20 pm (last
admission)
Sun: 12.30 pm–3.30 pm
(last admission)
April–September:
Mon–Sat:
9.30 am–5.00 pm (last
admission)
Sun: 11.00 am–5.00 pm
(last admission)

Price Guide: D

Car Parking:
Not permitted on
Esplanade.
Limited in surrounding
streets.

Where to eat:
Wide choice on Royal
Mile.

View over city from
Castle ramparts

Drawing the eye like a magnet up the spiky silhouette of the Old Town is Edinburgh Castle itself, standing on its stump of black basalt as if it had grown out of the very rock itself, peaceful now but for the steady tramp of sightseers' feet on its old cobbles.

A tour of exploration should start on the Esplanade, which isn't there simply to act as a coach park or the setting for the annual Military Tattoo. It has its own treasures which are well worth seeing before even going into the castle. There are several monuments along its north side, including the granite stone commemorating Ensign Ewart, one of General Tam Dalyell's men, who captured the French standard at the Battle of Waterloo in 1815. Carved on the stone is the French eagle which topped the standard, and which was later adopted as the badge of the Scots Greys, a regiment which has its own museum of relics at the top of the castle.

On the stone wall of the moat near the castle entrance, a plaque indicates a small piece of Scotland which belongs to Nova Scotia, a reciprocal arrangement made with that Canadian province.

Set into niches flanking the entrance gate are statues of Scotland's two national heroes, Sir William Wallace and King Robert the Bruce, while over the gate itself is the country's coat-of-arms which reads, translated: 'Wha' daur meddle wi' me'. The gatehouse itself is Victorian, a latter-day addition when it was felt that the castle deserved a more imposing entrance, and further up the cobbled road stands the original main gateway, Argyle Tower. Look upwards and you can see the great slit which houses the portcullis. Once inside the castle precincts, you come first to the Argyle Battery and the Mill's Mount Battery where the famous one o'clock gun is situated.

Pedestrians automatically check their watches when the gun is fired every day, a modern interpretation of its original purpose as an accurate time signal to shipping in the Forth estuary. In order that the signal could be seen as well as heard, depending on weather conditions, a ball mounted on top of Nelson's Monument high on Calton Hill is dropped as the gun is fired.

Further on towards the top citadel of the castle is the Forewall Battery, level with the roof of the Argyle Tower. The great defensive ramparts curve round to what is probably the most familiar of the batteries, the Half Moon. This is a distinctive feature of Edinburgh Castle, being built on the site of an earlier square tower known as King David's Tower, demolished during a seige in 1573.

The most famous gun at the castle ever to be fired in anger is Mons Meg, the $6\frac{1}{2}$-ton cannon which was built in 1449 in Belgium by order of Philip the Good, Duke of Burgundy. Costing him £1536, Mons Meg was originally installed at his castle in Lille before the Duke sent it to Scotland as a gift to the monarchy. For ammunition it used stone balls, each weighing five hundredweight, and when fired in 1558 to celebrate the marriage of Mary Queen of Scots to Francis, Dauphin of France, it is said that the cannonball used was found two miles away. Having eventually burst during a salute in 1680, the gun lay neglected until the 1750s when it was moved to the Tower of London, Sir Walter Scott securing its return to Edinburgh 80 years later.

Mons Meg was to go to London again, this time on a loan basis in 1984, when the ancient cannon underwent modern electronic tests by scientists to determine exactly how craftsmen of 500 years ago had managed to put together such a formidable piece of weaponry.

The cannon is now housed in the French prisons at the castle. These buildings once held the prisoners taken during the Napoleonic

Mons Meg, built in 1449

fine hammerbeam roof. This hall was the scene of the notorious Black Dinner when members of the Douglas family were invited to a meal, only to be murdered by their adversaries.

The remaining rooms in the Palace Block, with its tall clock tower, contain historical apartments associated with Mary Queen of Scots and James VI. In this building, too, are housed Scotland's greatest treasures: the Scottish Crown Jewels, comprising the crown, sceptre, and sword of state.

The crown was made for James V in 1540, but it is believed that the circlet may date from further back. The sceptre, a hexagonal rod of gilded silver, was a gift from Pope Alexander VI to James IV. It was remade in its present form for James V, and topped by a globe of rock crystals. The sword of state, crafted in the style of the Italian goldsmith Benvenuto Cellini, was presented to James IV in 1507 by Pope Julius II, together with an ornamental scabbard and belt.

Incredible though it may seem, the Honours of Scotland, to give the jewels their ancient name, were apparently lost for about 150 years. During Cromwell's period of power, they were removed from the castle for safety. When they were brought back in the latter 1660s, they were locked in an old oak chest and put in a room which was then sealed. It was due to the insistent efforts of Sir Walter Scott that a proper search was made, and the jewels once again saw the light of day.

Representing the continuity of the monarchy into the present day, the dazzling beauty of the Scottish Crown Jewels makes a fitting climax to a tour of the capital's castle.

Wars, the men being responsible for building the road which winds around the rock. At the top lies the tiny Norman chapel dedicated to St Margaret, still used for marriages by military personnel stationed at the castle.

Just below the parapet near the chapel is a little walled enclosure clinging to the rock. This is the Dogs' Cemetery, where small headstones mark the graves of garrison pets or regimental mascots buried there.

The imposing Scottish National War Memorial is in Crown Square. This moving record in bronze, stained glass and stone commemorates the Scottish war dead from the First World War onwards. The names of all Scots who died, armed or civilian, are listed on the great rolls of honour – carved on one wall there is even a memorial to the canaries used to detect gas in the trenches during World War I. A large part of Crown Square is given over to the Scottish United Services Museum, with uniforms, equipment and weapons on display.

Adjoining the War Memorial is the Great Hall, which has a collection of armour under its

The Castle Gate

THE GRASSMARKET

It was James III who, in 1477, decreed that various localities near the Old Town should be designated as weekly market sites for different trades. The motive was simply commercial, and no-one could possibly have envisaged the bloody depths to which the Grassmarket would sink during the next three hundred years.

Nestling under the precipitous south side of the Castle rock, the Grassmarket was a meeting place for farmers and carriers, and those connected with country cattle and horse markets. Old etchings show it to have been a spacious, busy area, with a variety of architecture in the surrounding buildings, most of which were topped with great chimneys and crow-stepped gables.

In 1543, the local council decided that the market should be paved, at the modest cost of 26s. 8d per rood. Today's Highways Department would no doubt have different ideas.

In about 1660 the friendly bustle of a country fair was replaced by a more sinister atmosphere when the site for public executions was moved from Castle Hill and Market Cross to the spacious area of the Grassmarket. Here many more of the populace could indulge their taste for this morbid entertainment, slaking their thirst during intervals at the Bow Foot Well, erected in 1681 and still there.

As well as common criminals, many Convenanters, those staunch defenders of the Protestant faith in Scotland, were to meet their end in this bloody human shambles, although to many it was probably a blessed release after their incarceration in Greyfriars churchyard, with no shelter and little food.

It is somewhat ironic that during the reign of Charles II the city hangman, one Alexander Cockburn, was himself executed here for murdering one of the King's men.

The tale of 'Half-hangit Maggie Dickson' is one which is still remembered locally. In 1724, she was tried for murdering her illegitimate child, and her plea that her husband was then working in Newcastle made no impression on the court. After the execution, Maggie's friends managed to escape the attentions of some surgeon-apprentices who wanted to avail themselves of the body, and set off home. However, the jolting of the cart in which the coffin lay had stirred Maggie's blood, renewed vitality, and by the time Musselburgh was reached, she had completely recovered. She spent her later years producing more children, keeping an ale-house, and selling salt in the streets of Edinburgh.

The rabble was not always satisfied with the way the entertainment was conducted, and 1736 saw one of the most famous riots ever to erupt in the Grassmarket. The mob apparently took exception to the hanging of a smuggler, one Andrew Wilson, so town guard Captain Porteous ordered his men to fire into the crowd, killing six people and wounding others.

The captain was tried and condemned for the killings, a royal reprieve serving only to further anger those who had seen their fellow men mown down. They set fire to the door of the Tolbooth, pulled the unfortunate man out, dragged him down to the Grassmarket, and proceeded to hang him from a pole lent by a dyer and with a rope taken from a nearby shop. The ringleaders were believed to be people of some importance, mingling with the mob, but they were never traced. The matter was raised in Parliament, the city was fined, and Mrs Porteous was given the money as a pension.

The last hanging to take place at the Grassmarket was that of a robber in 1784, but the huge stone base, hollowed out to take the foot of the gallows-tree, remained there for some years. It was eventually replaced by a Cross of St Andrew set into the roadway in rose-coloured stones to mark the spot.

Towards the end of the eighteenth century, the old inns were developing into more modern hostelries providing stabling, and mainly grouped at the town gates and in the Grassmarket area. Some of these, suitably modernised and on the north side, still serve their original purpose, the stables now being replaced by the relentless clicking of parking meters.

A few pleasant hours can be spent wandering around this old market place, with its assortment of small shops, cafes and ale-houses, as well as the equally interesting West Bow and Victoria Street which curve up to George IV Bridge. The energetic could, if so inclined, tackle the steep old stairs which climb up the cliffside to the Castle Esplanade.

Grassmarket Fair during the Festival

BURGLARS AND BODY-SNATCHERS

Every town has its legendary 'baddies', and one cannot delve into the seamy side of Edinburgh without remembering the three most reprehensible characters ever to sully its streets, Burke and Hare, and Deacon Brodie. So many stories surround them that it is difficult to decide where truth ends and imagination takes over, but whichever way you like to look at it, their escapades put them firmly into the history books.

Two Irish labourers, William Burke and William Hare, lived in a squalid den just off the Grassmarket. Their macabre career during the 1820s started when they realised that they could earn an easy £16 by supplying a corpse to surgeons doing research. Creeping out at night, they did the rounds of the local churchyards, robbing the newly-covered graves. As a result

many of the churchyards built watchtowers in which wardens kept guard.

After this setback, it didn't take them long to turn to murder as a more convenient means of supply. Legend has it that victims were lured to a cheap boarding house, plied with liquor until they were senseless, and then smothered. The murderers had one narrow escape when a medical student recognised the body of a young girl, but the evil trade ended only when visitors found one of their victims and called the police.

To avoid punishment, Hare turned King's Evidence, and betrayed his partner. Burke was hanged in the Lawnmarket in January 1829 – and his body was then taken, ironically, to the School of Anatomy for dissection.

Deacon Brodie, although he too turned to crime for financial gain, was on the face of it a highly respectable and respected citizen: a city councillor, with a flourishing cabinet-making business. His social life, however, was one long round of gambling, dice-playing, and drinking in the Old Town taverns. His greatest pleasure was cock-fighting, and it was reckless gambling at the cockpit which started him down the slippery path.

Taking advantage of his knowledge of Edinburgh society and business, he began to carry out a series of carefully planned burglaries under cover of darkness, using keys which he had forged from putty or clay impressions.

His secret life was unsuspected until he was betrayed after a raid on the city's Excise Offices. He fled to London and thence to Amsterdam with the idea of going on to America, but he made the fatal mistake of entrusting to a fellow-passenger some letters to be delivered in Edinburgh. His whereabouts became known to the authorities, and Brodie was brought home to stand trial. In 1788, a crowd of 40,000 went to see him hanged at the Tolbooth – on a gibbet he had designed himself. The crowd got a good show: twice he mounted the gallows, and twice it refused to work. The third time he was not so lucky, and Edinburgh's most notorious councillor was dead.

THE ROYAL MILE

The Royal Mile is inseparable from Edinburgh; it is as much part of the city as the castle or the palace of Holyroodhouse. It links the two along the rocky spine of the Old Town, and in so doing, it knits together the colourful and historic fabric of the capital's past and present.

Leading out from the Castle Esplanade on its downhill route to the palace, the Royal Mile really comprises five streets running one into another: Castlehill, Lawnmarket, High Street, Canongate, and Abbey Strand. The most enjoyable way of finding out all about such a fascinating street is to take plenty of time and do your own exploring on foot, combining what you see today with what you see through the mind's eye – using your imagination to picture these five streets as they may have looked many years ago.

The first houses on the Royal Mile would have been thatched wooden dwellings, probably no more than two storeys high, built with timber felled in Drumselch Forest. Immediately adjoining the Castle rock, the forest was King David I's favourite hunting ground. Most of the houses would comprise a shopping booth on the ground floor, with maybe only one room above reached by an outside stair. Glass-making was still unkown in Scotland; windows were simply holes cut in the walls.

By the 1500s, the Royal Mile was built-up from castle to abbey, punctuated by many closes giving entry to tenements, or courts surrounded by buildings. Access to these was through the archways known as pends. Some of the better-class houses were now of stone, and the burgesses who bought the Town Council's excess timber from tree-felling operations were allowed the privilege of extending their homes seven feet into the street, which didn't do much to help congestion in the already busy thoroughfare.

At the same time, the erection of the town wall known as the Flodden Wall, built in haste after that battle had been lost to the English, restricted the available building land still further as more people clamoured for safety within the fortifications. So the trend for building upwards began.

Many of the dilapidated earlier buildings were pulled down and rebuilt in stone, each containing often half-a-dozen homes in tall, narrow vertical villages, the forerunners of today's tenements, each block being known as a land. This was part of a general renovation of the Royal Mile. People began to paint their ceilings and walls; the rich hung tapestries. Thatched roofs and all-wood buildings were condemned; holes cut in wooden facings became windows; and outside stairs were no longer allowed to be built because of the narrowness of the street.

A number of existing outside stairs were allowed to remain, which was just as well, for most of the inside stairs were far too narrow to accommodate a coffin! So a law was passed allowing the late departed to be passed out through a window on to a convenient neighbour's outside stair, thence to be bumped down to the street.

Although an improvement to the basic look of the Old Town's main street, the new arrangements did have drawbacks for the residents, especially the more fastidious. With sanitation and running water still non-existent, the stench was abominable and earned Edinburgh the unenviable nickname of 'Auld Reekie'. A familiar cry to be heard in those times was 'Gardy-loo', an adaptation from the French meaning, in effect, 'watch yourself', as housewives prepared to empty the family garbage and waste into the street below, regardless of passers-by. The innocent pedestrian had to be quick to yell back 'haud yer hand' before the slops drenched his person.

Many of the older buildings had windows which were half glass and half wooden shutters, and these can still be seen on a number of the restored buildings. This goes back to the years between 1695 and 1850 when a tax was put on glass, a tax so severe that it was reckoned to take seven years to save up for a replacement pane – the origin of the present-day superstition that a broken mirror (or glass) brings seven

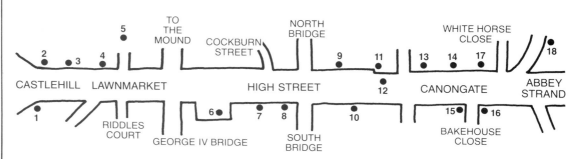

stones of its west wall is the cannonball which supposedly misfired when let off during the Jacobite siege of 1745. Some say it was placed there to mark the gravitation height of the city's first proposed water supply; others say it marks the limit of housebuilding to the castle walls.

Castlehill has a murky past, for it was the site of hundreds of executions, and many witches in particular met their end by being burned at the stake there, so it is a pleasant relief to walk into the wider reaches of the Lawnmarket. It was otherwise known as Land Market, and the country people whose stalls once thronged the street must have brought a breath of fresh air with them as well as the farm produce, meat, woollens and linen which they sold.

An insight into the trade of a cloth merchant can be gained at Gladstone's Land, the finest example of a seventeenth-century high-rise block to survive in the Royal Mile, with its arcaded ground floor, shopping booths, and outside stone spiral stair leading from the pavement to the main door for the upper storeys. Now in the care of the National Trust for Scotland, much of the building has been restored and refurnished with carefully-selected antique pieces in a reconstruction of a typical house of the period.

Originally built around 1550 or earlier, the six-storey stone and timber house was bought by local merchant Thomas Gledstanes in 1617, who promptly proceeded to do what most of his neighbours were already doing – extending his property by adding the arcade, topped by new rooms on the front of each floor. In this way he assisted in the fashionable pastime of making the Lawnmarket even narrower than it was before.

years' bad luck. And with that sort of taxation, no wonder the poorer people had to make do with pigskins to keep out the elements.

There was still some time to go before the advent of sewers, street cleaning, water supplies and lighting, but by the 1700s the general architectural pattern of the Royal Mile as we know it today began to emerge.

The houses clinging like limpets to the north rockface at the start of Castlehill are the first in the Royal Mile. Now mainly converted into prestigious flats, they look particularly picturesque when seen perched on the skyline from the lower level of Princes Street. The most unusual was that built for wigmaker-turned-bookseller, Allan Ramsay. All its rooms were octagonal, giving the whole structure such a peculiarly round shape that it became known as Guse-pie, or Goose-pie. Succeeding occupants enlarged and altered the premises, which are now used by a business company. Perhaps that is why Allan Ramsay stands with his back to it on his statue plinth in Princes Street Gardens.

Also at the top of Castlehill, at its junction with Castle Wynd North, is Cannonball House dating from 1630. Wedged among the rough

Gladstone's Land

The arcades at street level were built to accommodate two shopping booths, and behind them can be seen the lines of the original frontage. The first booth as one enters the building is a replica of a cloth merchants' shop, showing old tools of the trade and displaying fabrics representing the hand-spun and woven woollens of the 1600s, coloured with basic vegetable dyes from plants gathered in the hedgerows and fields.

A turnpike stair at the rear twists its way up the full height of the house, giving access at each level to the living quarters. Only the more important floors are open to the public. Some of the rooms are especially noteworthy for the intricately painted beamed ceilings, similar to The Study at Culross, and reflecting again the Scandinavian influence which sea trade with those countries brought to the east of Scotland.

Lady Stair's House and Close

Gladstone's Land

These ceilings, together with some wall decoration, were hidden by layers of paint and plaster until discovered in 1934 when a rescue operation was launched to save what had degenerated into a condemned slum, and restore Gladstone's Land to its former dignity as the home of a well-to-do city merchant and his prosperous tenants.

A few paces away, still on the north side, an archway leads to a quiet close with a sombre

black lamp-post standing sentinel over Lady Stair's House. Built in 1622 by Sir William Grey of Pittendrum for his wife, it still has a door lintel bearing the date and their initials, although much of the house has been considerably altered. Acquired by the Earl of Rosebery in 1895 and restored, the house was presented to the city and now houses relics of Scott, Stevenson, and Burns.

Across the road on the south side are the two archways leading into Riddle's Court and a fine collection of buildings whose architecture spans more than 300 years. Directly in front of the visitor is the house built in the late 1500s by one of the wealthiest local citizens of the time, Bailie John McMorran, a magistrate and town councillor.

Unfortunately, the good Bailie met an untimely end while attending to his duty in both capacities. The High School was at that time the responsibility of the Town Council, and when the boys staged a sit-in because they had been refused a holiday, Bailie McMorran, aided by a handful of constables, was sent to the school as arbiter.

The more he persuaded, the more stubborn the boys became, and when the Bailie and his men attempted to ram down the door, one of the pupils threatened to let off his pistol. In the false belief that it was mere bluff, Bailie McMorran continued his ramming attempts and was rewarded by a bullet through the head.

Bailie McMorran's house remained in the family, and a few years later the splendid mansion was lent to the Town Council for the banquet given in honour of King James VI and Queen Anne during a visit to Edinburgh. As well as the many fine foods and entertainments – which, no doubt, were eventually paid for by the long-suffering ratepayers – the accounts for the banquet included £8 for providing linen napkins, all of which somehow disappeared during the evening!

The Lawnmarket eventually becomes the High Street, having been intersected by George IV Bridge at its junction with the top of the Mound. The top end of High Street is the city's legal and administrative centre, overshadowed by the bulk of St Giles Cathedral.

In Parliament Square, guarded by the Mercat Cross, can be found the district court and the Court of Session; the Parliament Hall which was used by Scottish politicians before the Union in 1707, and now a legal waiting-room for lawyers from the adjacent courts; and the headquarters of Lothian Regional Council.

On the other side of High Street are the pillars fronting the forecourt of the Edinburgh City Chambers. Originally built in 1761 as a Royal Exchange, the new centre of commerce was not particularly well received by the city merchants, more accustomed to conducting their business transactions out in the street! It has been used as a council chamber since 1811.

The importance of this little patch of the capital is emphasised by the design of cobbles laid in the road near St Giles – the Heart of Midlothian. This is no mere decoration, however, but the site of the door of the condemned cell in the old Tolbooth which stood on that place from 1346 until 1817. A not unusual sight is that of a passer-by spitting on the Heart. This is no

The Heart of Midlothian

disrespect to its symbolism but an almost forgotten tradition that passers-by used to spit on the door of the airless, waterless, drainless Tolbooth in the sincere hope that they would never enter it. The plan of the Tolbooth is also marked out in tiles on the roadway.

There are many intriguing closes down the rest of High Street, all bearing the ancient nameplates which indicate who lived there, or what trade was followed. To continue into the lower half of High Street, one must cross the other intersecting road where the North and South Bridges meet.

A little way down on the north side is an interesting memorial: a sculpture of a boy's face surmounted by an inscription. One November morning in 1861, three High Street tenements suddenly crashed to the ground, killing 35 people. As they cleared the rubble, rescuers heard a trapped boy shouting: 'Heave awa' chaps, I'm no dead yet', and those words were incorporated into the carving.

Apart from the castle itself, the most famous building in Edinburgh, if not Scotland, must be John Knox's house. Built around 1490, it started life as a typical town house two storeys high with a basement below street level. Later additions combined to achieve the quaintness of its overhanging upper floors, crow-stepped gables, and outside stair which give the house its appeal, as well as the miscellany of small shops which have always occupied the ground and basement floors.

Records show that the original residents were a family named Arres. One of their descendants was to marry goldsmith James Mossman (son of the jeweller who fashioned the Scottish crown) who, after taking up the appointment of Assaye of the Mint to Mary Queen of Scots, was later executed for his allegiance to the monarch and her faith.

Although the house is traditionally regarded as the home of John Knox, he had a number of other residences long since demolished, and various theories have been put forward as to the length of time he actually spent here. Tradition dies hard, though, and the renovated house is now a museum and memorial to the great reformer.

A little further past John Knox's House, the High Street ends where brass plates in the roadway outline the site of the Netherbow Port. Originally an arched gateway with a clocktower and spire, this was one of the six gates which could seal off entry to the old town of Edinburgh.

John Knox's House

Originally built in 1513 and part of the Flodden Wall, the Netherbow Port was yet another victim of Hertford's invasion in 1544. It was rebuilt, and stood until the more peaceful times of the latter 1700s when it was demolished to allow a clear passage from the High Street into Canongate. In its time, the Netherbow also served to introduce a cautionary note into the minds of those passing through its gate, for the heads of executed criminals and dissident preachers were stuck up on spikes on the gate as a warning to all.

Until 1856, when it was absorbed into the Royal Burgh of Edinburgh, the Canongate remained a burgh in its own right, granted that status and taking its name from the road (or gait) used by David I's monks as they walked between Holyrood and the Old Town.

Being outside the protection of the town walls and away from the seething masses of humanity further up the Royal Mile, Canongate only began to expand when James IV started to build the palace adjoining the abbey, and the Scottish nobility felt it was the 'in thing' to start putting up their smart homes as near as possible to their monarch.

In many ways, that was their undoing. They found themselves unprotected during invasions; left high and dry after the Scottish Court moved to London in 1603 after the Union of the Crowns; and neglected still further when the Scottish Parliament followed suit in 1707. The final exodus of the wealthier householders to the greener pastures of the New Town in the 1770s was too much for the Canongate, and it slid rapidly into decline.

Fortunately for present and future generations, a great deal of restoration work done during the last few decades has brought most of the street back into the category of desirably residential, the sympathetic architecture of the recent structures blending well with the old and historic buildings.

Above the arch of Mid Common Close, on the north side of the Canongate, is a quaint little effigy of a Moor – something one does not quite expect to find in the Scottish capital. The story behind it is unexpected, too, but enjoyable.

In about 1640, a young student called Andrew Grey rebelled against Charles I's attempts to introduce the English prayer book into the Scots kirk, insulted the provost, and tried to burn his house down. Sentenced to death, he was put in the Tolbooth prison but mysteriously disappeared the night before his execution.

A few years later, during the great plague of 1645, a Moorish ship docked at Leith and its crew marched up the Canongate to demand entry at the Netherbow. Their leader turned out to be Andrew Grey, who after his escape had found his way to Morocco and found sufficient favour with the sultan to be lent a ship to come back for his revenge on Edinburgh.

The Netherbow Port, from an early 18th century drawing

White Horse Close

Given the option of having the city burnt down or handing over a considerable ransom, the senior citizens conceded the latter, their manpower too depleted by the plague to be able to fight. Still not content, Andrew Grey demanded the provost's son as a hostage. On learning that the provost only had a daughter, herself ill, Grey said he had an elixir from the east which would cure her. She was brought to a house in the Canongate, where Grey nursed her, cured her, and – you've guessed it – married her. With the money he had received from the city, Grey built his house, put up a statue to his Moorish benefactor, and called it Moroccoland, a name which has stuck to this day.

One of the most important historic buildings in the Canongate is the city's local history museum at Huntly House, which will be found in the Museums section, together with the adjoining Bakehouse Close and Acheson House.

Opposite Huntly House is the Canongate Tolbooth, not to be confused with the now demolished Tolbooth of the High Street. This building, with its spire, projecting turret room, outside stair and enormous clock, was built in the late 1500s to collect road tolls. It also saw service as the council chamber, courtroom and gaol of the Burgh of Canongate. It is now used to house various local exhibitions, and there is a brass rubbing centre on the ground floor.

Almost at the foot of the Canongate is the familiar White Horse Close. Apart from being displayed prominently on the label of a well-known brand of whisky, White Horse Close has more serious claims to fame. In the sixteenth century, conveniently situated just beyond the sacred precincts of the Abbey Strand, it was the humble home of the Royal Mews. The White Horse Inn itself, and the adjacent coaching stables, were built in 1623 by Burgess Laurence

Ord, who named his hostelry after Mary Queen of Scots' white palfrey. From the back, or shall we say the tradesmen's entrance, the stagecoach left for Newcastle and London, a total mammoth journey of eight days which cost five pounds.

During the occupation of Edinburgh by Bonnie Prince Charlie's army in 1745, the Prince lorded it at Holyrood while his Jacobite officers made merry at the inn which they used as their headquarters.

Not surprisingly, there was a blacksmith's forge in the close. This belonged to the father of William Dick, born there in 1793, the founder of Edinburgh's Veterinary College which is now affectionately known as the Dick Vet.

The last few yards of the Royal Mile take you into the Abbey Strand and Sanctuary. The sixteenth-century buildings on the north side once formed part of a so-called residence for aristocratic debtors, in which they were safe from arrest within the sanctuary afforded not only by the buildings but by Holyrood Park and Arthur's Seat as well. Part of the block has now been converted for use by court officials during royal visits.

Do not for one minute imagine that these are the only places to see in the Royal Mile. After all, *Explore Edinburgh* is an invitation to do just that; it does not pretend to be a comprehensive guidebook, but simply tries to point the reader in the right direction. Depending on where one's interest lies, and excluding all the closes which are worthy of investigation, and the many specialist shops, look out for the following: the Camera Obscura and Outlook Tower, the Museum of Childhood, the Edinburgh Wax Museum, the Netherbow Arts Centre, the Tron Kirk, the Scottish Crafts Centre and the Canongate Church and churchyard.

HOLYROOD

Holyrood Abbey

Legends inextricable weave their threads between the facts of history, and the story of the founding of the Abbey of Holyrood is no exception.

One day in 1128 King David I, then living at Edinburgh Castle and having attended a mass on the feast of the Exaltation of the Holy Cross, was persuaded by the younger element of his court to go out hunting in his favourite Drumselch Forest near the castle. This expedition considerably displeased his confessor Alwin, an English canon.

As the hunt approached Salisbury Crag, the King was charged by a great stag which succeeded in throwing him off his horse and wounding him in the leg. David made a grab at the stag as he fell, and found himself clutching a crucifix which had suddenly glowed between its antlers; meanwhile the animal made off in the direction of a spring of water where it had first appeared.

That night, the King dreamed that he heard a strange voice call his name three times, adding that he should 'make a house for Canons devoted to the Cross'. So vivid was the dream that David did as he had been bidden, and erected the Augustinian monastery of Holy Rood (or Holy Cross) near the spring where the stag had materialised.

This legend is commemorated by the stag's head bearing a cross which is carved on nearby later buildings, and the motif was also incorporated into the official seals of the ancient abbots of Holyrood.

Lying within what was then a forest setting, the abbey thrived and became prosperous. Conforming to the traditional monastery plan, the abbey kirk and domestic quarters surrounded the cloisters; the guest house and infirmary lay alongside within the precinct wall. Of the several gateways, the main entrance faced towards the town along the Canons' Gait (gait being the old Scots word for road). Under David's Charter to Holyrood this area was granted to the canons as their own burgh, Canongate, and it retained its individual burgh status until 1856 when it became absorbed into the city.

All that survives of those early buildings are geometrical designs in the lawns, and what today's visitor sees are the remains of the abbey's ruined nave. Its decline dates from 1544, when Hertford and his English troops desecrated the abbey, returning three years later to strip the lead coverings from the roof. In 1569 the General Assembly of the Reformed Kirk ordered the demolition of the transepts, chapels and presbytery, after which the nave was repaired to serve the parish of the Canongate.

King Charles I, in his fervour for episcopacy, enthusiastically produced restoration plans in the 1600s, one of which was to roof over the vaulted ceilings with great stone slabs. That proved to be the final straw for the old abbey; the weight of the stone was just too much for the structure and in 1768 the roof collapsed, leaving the ruins as they are today, a great tracery of arches open to the sky.

The palace of Holyroodhouse began its life as the obligatory guest house attached to the abbey. Scots kings lodged there during occasional visits, and it was to provide the nucleus from which the present palace grew, added to and re-built by succeeding monarchs.

James IV extended the guest house in 1501 for himself, and James V built the north-west tower of Holyrood as a royal apartment to replace older quarters. Damaged during the English invasions of the 1540s, and again by a fire in Cromwell's time, Holyroodhouse only began to take on today's aspect when Charles II commissioned the services of architect Sir William Bruce. Prudently taking his lead from the Court of St James and their known preference for the purer classical styles, Sir William blended Roman Doric, Ionic and Corinthian architecture to present Scotland with its first major classical building.

Palace of Holyroodhouse

Open:
October–May:
Mon–Sat:
9.30 am–4.30 pm
Sun: 12.30 pm–4.30 pm
June–September:
Mon–Sat:
9.30 am–6.00 pm
Sun: 11.0 am–6.00 pm

From second week of May to mid-June, the State and Historical Apartments are closed for the visit of the Lord High Commissioner to the General Assembly of the Church of Scotland. The Palace may be closed at short notice for periods of residence by the Royal Family and for State Visits.

Price Guide: C

Car Parking:
Free parking area on south side of Palace within Holyrood Park.

Where to eat:
Tea Room near main gate open during summer months.
Wide choice in Royal Mile

Robert Mylne, the King's Master Mason, descended from a family who had held that office for generations, was given the task of building the palace. Between 1671 and 1676 the giant jigsaw was put together, and at long last, James IV's original idea that a south tower should set off the frontage came to fruition. The medieval tower, where the apartments associated with Mary Queen of Scots are situated, was retained and incorporated into the new design, involving considerable adjustments of floor levels, windows and doors.

Despite Charles II's interest in Holyroodhouse, he was never destined to live there, and for nearly 100 years it lay neglected until the explosive arrival of Bonnie Prince Charlie who moved into his ancestral home during the 1740s on a temporary basis, putting life into the palace with great balls, entertainments, and assemblies.

During his state visit in 1822 King George IV – the first British monarch to visit Edinburgh for 200 years – held a levee in the palace, and although he did not take up residence, this gesture was sufficient to ensure Holyrood's restoration to royal favour.

Queen Victoria and Prince Albert used the royal apartments, frequently staying at the palace on their journeys to and from Balmoral. The state apartments with their fine eighteenth-century furniture, and their French and Flemish tapestries, are said to have given Queen Victoria great pleasure.

The fountain in the forecourt was erected by Queen Victoria, based on the design used by James V for his fountain at the palace of Linlithgow. The Queen also gave her name to the carriageway which encircles Holyrood Park. The magnificent sets of wrought-iron gates at the three entrances to the palace forecourt were erected in 1920 as the nation's memorial to King Edward VII.

So the royal links with Scotland were finally and irrevocably forged. The pattern was set which has been followed by monarchs throughout this century, placing the palace of Holyroodhouse firmly where it belongs as a living, breathing family home, the Scottish palace of the British monarchy.

QUEEN MARY'S BATH

Bath house, summer house, quiet retreat for sewing or reading? No-one will ever know now, but the tiny building in a former garden not far from the main palace gates rarely fails to intrigue people, if for no other reason than because it juts out into the pavement and one has to walk round it!

Generally known as Queen Mary's Bath, it is a quaint triangular structure with a pointed roof and the minimum of windows. It has been dated as early seventeenth-century, for at that time it was usual to build small pavilions at the corners of enclosed gardens. If there was a convenient stream, these pavilions were sometimes used for bathing; otherwise they were more likely to be used as summer houses, part of the miniature architecture which adds such interest to formal gardens.

HOLYROOD PARK

A few hours spent in Holyrood Park makes pleasant relaxation for all ages. A delight to the children feeding ducks; a mini-mountaineering expedition for the more energetic; a paradise for geologists or bird-watchers; or just somewhere to go to blow away the cobwebs.

Arthur's Seat, the highest of the seven ancient volcanoes on which Edinburgh grew up, towers over the city like the great lion it is said to resemble, crouched in the middle of the park. Every few yards show evidence of the massive volcanic and glacial activity which combined to produce the present geological jigsaw, helped by weather erosion which has laid bare the many different rock strata.

The origins of its name are unknown, but there are many legends over which to speculate. It has been suggested that the Seat was named after King Arthur of Strathclyde, slain in the 500s at the Battle of Camelon near Falkirk. This no doubt is where confusion arises with King Arthur of Camelot, an improbable candidate since it is extremely unlikely that he ever ventured so far north.

An alternative theory suggests that the name derives from the Gaelic *Ard-na-Saigheid*, meaning the height of a flight of arrows; perhaps it was once used as a practice ground by archers? The truth will probably never be known.

Facts which cannot be denied are that Arthur's Seat was used for location shots during the making of the Sean Connery film *From Russia With Love*; and also that Anneka Rice found herself temporarily stranded on the summit during an episode of ITV's *Treasure Hunt*!

At one time the park, which covers about 650 acres, was within the boundaries of the ancient sanctuary of Holyrood Abbey, and a man could be safe here from his creditors for 24 hours. In 1540, the park was enclosed by James V as part of Holyroodhouse grounds, and it was then known as King's or Queen's Park because, according to Sir Walter Scott, it was 'dedicated to the preservation of the royal game'.

During the great plague which ravaged the city in 1645, the park took on another role, that of a great open-air hospital to which the sick were sent. Despite being given some sort of medical attention, many died and were buried on the spot.

Holyrood Park has three entrances, the main one being beside the palace. The park is encircled by Queen's Drive, a one-way road named after Queen Victoria. Starting the circuit here, one comes first to St Margaret's Well, dedicated to the wife of Malcolm III. Built in the fifteenth century, it formerly stood near Restalrig, where it was inconveniently in the way of a proposed railway station. It was transferred in its entirety to the present site in 1862, on the north face of the Salisbury Crags, overhung by a solitary tree.

On a nearby knoll overlooking the artificially-made St Margaret's Loch is the ruin of St Anthony's Chapel and the adjacent hermitage, dating from around 1430. Little is known about the original building, but there is thought to be some connection with the Preceptory of St Anthony at Leith, founded by

James I at around the same time. This seems reasonable, as the Leith hospital was for the treatment of erysipelas, then known as St Anthony's fire, and not far away from the chapel in the park there is a mineral spring bearing the same name.

Continuing round Whinney Hill, formed of at least 13 lava flows cooled into individual cliffs interspersed with grassy hollows, the road passes the secluded Dunsapie Loch, nestling under Dunsapie Hill. A path from the car park here provides the easiest, but still stiff, climb to the summit of Arthur's Seat with its indicator board which pinpoints landmarks as far distant as the Highlands.

Once past the Lion's Haunch and through a bouldered cutting, the thick lava shelf of Salisbury Crags is revealed. From this point in the road, a path known as the Radical Road follows the base of the cliffs round to the Holyroodhouse entrance. The Radical Road takes its name from the political views of the men who laid it in the years following the Napoleonic Wars, when there was high unemployment and increasing unrest among the workers. It was largely Sir Walter Scott who was behind the 1820 project to improve the old track and at the same time usefully dissipate the energies of potential trouble-makers.

On completion of the Radical Road, it was suggested that the nearby Samson's Ribs, the dramatic rock formation of six-sided columns five feet in diameter and 60 feet long, similar to the Giants' Causeway in Ireland, should be turned into a show garden with additional paths for hill walkers.

This was opposed by the Earl of Haddington, then hereditary Keeper of the Royal Park, with the excuse that it would upset the grazing sheep. This excuse, however, fell flat when he reopened the quarries on the crags and started selling the stone for paving the streets of London. So great was public indignation at this outrage that, in 1843, the park was handed over to the Commissioners of Woods and Forest, so ending commercial exploitation of the crags for all time.

There are two other park exits to select apart from that near the palace. Before completing the circuit, a left-hand junction takes you on to the older road to Duddingston, passing the wildlife sanctuary of the loch before emerging into the old village itself.

Alternatively, complete the circuit and, passing St Margaret's Loch again, leave by the straight road which exits into London Road. At this exit is a structure with a story. Known as Muschat's Cairn, it was built near the spot where a surgeon, Nicol Muschat, murdered his wife in 1720 by cutting her throat, previous attempts at divorce and poisoning having failed to relieve him of this apparent encumbrance!

St Giles

Few places of worship can have suffered as much turbulence during their history – including a riot among the congregation during one service – than St Giles, the High Kirk of Edinburgh, whose great bulk dominates the Royal Mile.

There has been a church on this site in the High Street since AD 854, when a small group of monks from Lindisfarne Priory in Northumberland built themselves a wooden chapel. This was replaced in the twelfth century by a considerably larger church, of which all that remains now are the four huge central pillars, survivors of an English attack in 1385. Subsequent years saw much rebuilding, including

inside and removing all the tombstones.

Years of religious rivalry followed, and at one time St Giles contained as many as four different churches within its great walls. Not only that, it also housed mundane secular institutions, such as a police station in the nave.

In 1633, the church was declared an episcopal cathedral, the partitions were removed, and it became as one again – for a short time. Four years later, when the unfortunate Dean Hanna of St Giles stood up to deliver the first-ever service from the specially-prepared episcopal prayer book insisted upon by Charles I, the congregation erupted, cabbage-seller Jenny Geddes so far forgetting herself as to throw her stool at the preacher. Episcopacy only survived another two years before it was abolished as the prescribed faith. Up went the partition walls again, and in 1689 Presbyterianism was established as the approved form of worship.

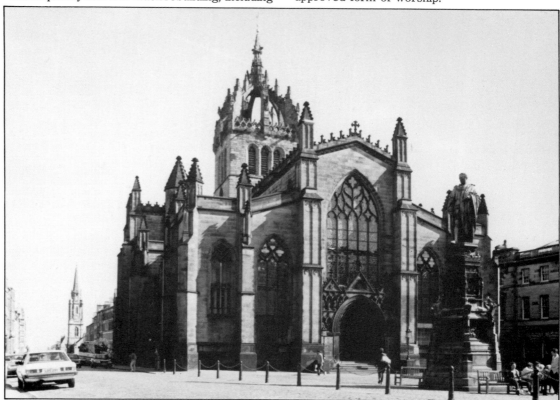

the addition of five chapels and a stone roof. In the mid-1400s the roof was raised, windows put in, and extensions pushed out. The 161-foot crown spire was completed in 1495.

John Knox, the great religious reformer, was to preach his first sermon in St Giles in 1559, and with the coming of the reform movement the 44 altars gifted by merchants, neighbouring lairds and craftsmen were seen as idolatory and promptly destroyed. The following year, John Knox became minister of the city, and he and his followers called on the services of sailormen from Leith to clear St Giles of all traces of the former order, even to the extent of whitewashing the

Major renovations to the exterior of St Giles were carried out in about 1830 when, much to the consternation of many of the town's citizens, the rubble-built walls were hidden behind a cladding of smooth grey masonry, the old tower and spire being the only parts unadulterated by the so-called improvements.

An important latter-day addition was made in 1911 with the opening of the newly-built Thistle Chapel. This is used on ceremonial occasions by the 16 members of Scotland's oldest order of chivalry, the Knights of the Thistle, an order which dates back to the time of James VII in 1687, if not earlier.

Gladstone's Land on the Royal Mile

Nelson's Monument on Calton Hill

PRINCES STREET GARDENS

There is no doubt that Princes Street is the most beautiful thoroughfare in the world, bounded as it is on one side by fine shops and on the other by the gentle slopes of Princes Street Gardens, which shelter under the towering cliffs of the old town and the castle.

These are gardens to be used and enjoyed, as indeed they were centuries ago when the valley was the King's Garden and a tournament ground. Today, office workers take their packed lunches, families take their picnics, and the chances are the cheeky pigeons will take both.

been prohibited on the south side of Princes Street, and the west gardens were being laid out, followed 15 years later by the east gardens.

The advent of rail travel was to cause problems, because as planned, the line would run straight through the gardens. After much opposition, the railway was eventually laid below the level of the gardens in tunnels and culverts.

A move to make the gardens public came in 1850 and a few years later the first band concerts were held. These were as popular then as they are now, and the original bandstand was erected in 1878, to be later replaced by today's Ross Bandstand and open-air theatre.

Programmes in the theatre have advanced considerably since those occasional band concerts, and during the summer months there are usually three or four different entertainments every day throughout the week. Bands still dominate the programme in keeping with

It seems strange to us now to realise that for more than 300 years it was a vast sheet of water, the Nor' Loch, artificially created as part of the town's defences in 1460 by damming the burn which ran through the valley. The Nor' Loch was the setting for all manner of strange edicts and events. Butchers and slaughterers were banned from dumping their offal; breakers of the Seventh Commandment were 'dookit' (ducked); the swans were ordered a special ration of oats; and on one occasion thousands of eels found themselves stranded on the banks after a storm.

The late 1700s saw the beginning of the end for the Nor' Loch. By then, James Craig's plan for the New Town was taking shape and work started on draining the Loch. This was completed in 1820. By then, building had already

tradition, but pop music, old time, sequence and country dancing provide almost non-stop variety. There is also Children's Hour each morning, with its Punch and Judy shows, magicians, puppets and music.

Sitting in the gardens facing the Old Town clinging to its ridge, one can see the imposing facade of the Assembly Hall in Mound Place where the General Assembly of the Church of Scotland gathers in May each year.

Also to the right of the Mound can be seen the ever-colourful face of the Floral Clock, measuring nearly 12 feet across – a pleasing complement to the classic columns of the Royal Scottish Academy and the National Gallery of Scotland.

STATUESQUE EDINBURGH

Walter Scott Memorial

There can surely be few city centres which boast such an abundance of monuments and statues within a relatively small area. In both the New and Old Towns, one can hardly turn a street corner without coming face-to-face with one dignitary or another, whether he be seated, standing, or astride a faithful steed.

Most people accept these memorials as part of the scenery, and would be hard put to give names to them, but there is one, of course, whose cathedral-like proportions are known throughout the world as epitomising the Scottish capital – the Scott Monument.

Four years after Sir Walter Scott died at his Borders home, the competition for the design of his memorial caused a considerable upheaval when it was won by the hitherto unknown George Meikle Kemp, a self-taught joiner and draughtsman, an obviously inferior personage to the eminent architects of the time who had also entered the contest.

Inspired by Melrose Abbey and Gothic memorial crosses, Kemp designed the 200-foot monument in only five days, and the foundation stone was laid in 1840 on a bed of solid rock 52 feet below street level in Princes Street Gardens.

So massive are the supporting pillars of this familiar landmark that one encloses a staircase leading to the series of look-out galleries – if you can manage the 287 steps! – and the Museum Room containing a number of interesting relics.

The statue of Sir Walter, sitting with a plaid over one shoulder and his dog, Maida, at his right foot, was the first marble effigy in Scotland, carved from a solid block of Carrera marble weighing 30 tons. Less imposing, but equally fascinating, are the 16 statuettes of other poets, and the 64 characters from Scott's novels which decorate the exterior.

Princes Street and its Gardens were obvious sites for many statues of local and national figures. Allan Ramsay, the wig-maker turned poet and bookseller, is rather unkindly depicted wearing a silk nightcap, the temporary substitute for a wig which was worn by gentlemen of his time in the privacy of their own homes. Still on the literary theme is the bronze statue of Adam Black, publisher and politician, Lord Provost for five years and also a Liberal Member of Parliament.

Of more modern memory is the Scottish American War Memorial erected in 1927 by Americans of Scottish descent to honour the Scottish effort in the Great War. Depicting a seated kilted soldier, bare-headed, rifle across his knees, this statue was protected by sandbags as a precaution against possible damage during the Second World War.

Scottish American War Memorial

The only statue in the gardens to be sculpted by a woman is that of Dr David Livingstone who, after his successful African explorations, was made an honorary burgess of Edinburgh. An explorer of somewhat chillier climes, Sir John Ross, has a fountain in his honour; this was no doubt regarded as more suitable given his preference for the polar regions.

Doctor Livingstone

Along Princes Street to its junction with Leith Walk is Register House, noted for its remarkable domed ceiling, and built by Robert Adam with money from forfeited Jacobite estates. Here are kept all Scotland's historical and legal archives, some dating back to the thirteenth century. The more mundane records of births, deaths and marriages are next door at New Register House.

On guard outside is the Duke of Wellington. Instead of being passively astride his mount, he sits on a prancing steed who is cleverly using his tail as the balancing point – a feat yet to be demonstrated at the Horse of the Year Show.

This was among the first of many statues to use the tail as a means of support, a device often used by sculptor Sir John Steell. All credit, too, to Sir John who, being unable to use the Duke's real warhorse Copenhagen as a model, borrowed a horse from the Duke of Buccleuch's stables at Dalkeith – a subterfuge he again used when sculpting the Albert Statue for Charlotte Square.

Round the corner from Register House is St Andrew Square, known as the richest square in Europe because of the number of British and international finance houses operating from there. Overlooking all this wealth is the tall column bearing the statue of Henry Dundas, the first Viscount Melville, who by the age of only 24 had achieved the post of Solicitor General for Scotland before rising through the political ranks to become First Lord of the Admiralty.

Outside the City Chambers in High Street is another of Sir John Steell's prancing horse statues. This is thought to be the Macedonian king Alexander taming his warhorse, and the huge work of art – the first bronze to be cast in Scotland – had to be moved some years ago from its original site in St Andrew Square as it had become a hazard to increasing road traffic.

In nearby Parliament Square is the oldest equestrian statue in Britain. Dated 1685 and of unknown origin, it depicts Charles II on his horse. Owing to lack of technical know-how on the part of the sculptors, the unfortunate animal has a tendency to buckle at the knees, necessitating fairly frequent surgery.

For many years the 1906 cast of John Knox stared rather aggressively across the square at the Merry Monarch's efforts to stay in the saddle. For those who wonder where he may have disappeared to, in 1983 he was taken off his pedestal and re-sited inside St Giles – ironically the very place where he had campaigned so vigorously against graven images in churches.

The Duke of Wellington

These are but a few of Edinburgh's many memorials, which together help to build up a picture of the men from all professions who were destined to be remembered in the city, and their contributions to its heritage.

Statues aren't merely lumps of stone, marble or metal. Look again, examine the folds of the clothes the sculptor so carefully chiselled; see how they stand and what they may be carrying. All these point to a way of life which is over and done with, but which helped to mould the pattern of our lives today.

CALTON HILL

High above the east end of Princes Street, with extensive views towards the Pentlands on one hand and Leith on the other, is the motley assortment of edifices which make up Calton Hill.

Looking rather as if a giant child had scattered a handful of his toys on the 355-foot hump of the hill, the area is dotted with Grecian-style buildings by various architects, creating the neo-Classical effect which earned Edinburgh the nickname 'Athens of the North'.

One of the most prominent neo-classical buildings is the cross-shaped New Observatory in Roman Doric style, whose dome dominates the hill. (It should not be confused with the space-age technology of the Royal Observatory, on Blackford Hill.) The New Observatory, naturally enough, was built to replace the Old Observatory, designed in 1776 but not finished until 1792. This was planned to resemble a fortress, being not much more than a tower with Gothic windows.

Appropriately nearby is a Grecian Doric monument to John Playfair, mathematician and one-time president of the Astronomical Institution.

Dugald Stewart, professor of moral philosophy at the university in 1785, is honoured by a memorial in the shape of a small circular temple, with nine fluted Corinthian pillars supporting the cupola and a carved urn in its centre. This is said to have been copied from the monument of Lysicrates in Athens, as is the memorial to Burns, further down the hill and across Regent Road.

A Crimean War Russian Gun

Pushing its tower skywards in representation of an upended telescope is the 108-foot-high Nelson Monument, erected between 1806 and 1819, and from which a time ball ascends and descends at one pm daily to coincide with the firing of the One o'Clock Gun from the Castle Battery.

The most striking of the structures, however, is the unfinished memorial to the Scottish soldiers and sailors who died in the Napoleonic Wars. Originally intended to be a copy of the Parthenon, funds ran out when only 12 of the soaring columns had been built. So it stands now, eye-catching certainly but pathetically smaller than the great church with catacombs which was dreamed of so many years ago.

On a suitably menacing vantage point is the Russian cannon captured at Sebastopol during the Crimean War, now aimed sternly but harmlessly over the city.

What was once the home of the Royal High School is perched on the south side of Calton Hill in Regent Road. The school was originally founded in the twelfth century under the supervision of the abbots of Holyrood. A new building was considered necessary by the city

fathers in the early 1800s, and a former pupil, Thomas Hamilton, was invited to submit a design. The result is now regarded as the most classical of the neo-Grecian edifices, the central hall being a copy of the Temple of Theseus in Athens.

After 1969, when the co-educational Royal High School at Barnton was opened, the old school lost its original function. It was used as the Civic Arts Centre for a few years, but such is the size and dignity of the building that it was earmarked as the venue for the proposed Scottish Parliament, and work began on refurbishing it in readiness for its new role. Unfortunately for the nationalistically-minded this was never to come about, as by the referendum of 1979 the electorate rejected the devolution proposals. The imposing building now houses the Scottish Crown Office, and the magnificent Assembly Hall is used only occasionally.

At the foot of the hill and on the other side of Regent Road once stood the Old Calton Jail, but it disappeared early this century (after the opening of the present Saughton Prison) to make way for St Andrew's House, Scotland's answer to Whitehall, which opened just before the Second World War. Of the prison, only the ruins of the governor's house remain, a small castle-like structure clinging like a fly to the hillside. It is said that the condemned cell was incorporated into the basement at St Andrew's House, but fortunately, is now used only for storage!

Nearby in the Old Calton Burial Ground with its beautifully-kept headstones, stands the first-ever statue of Abraham Lincoln to have been erected outside the USA: a double tribute to both the President and the Scottish soldiers who died in the American Civil War.

Surprisingly few pedestrians hurrying along Princes Street bother to lift up their eyes to Calton Hill. To the present generation it's there, always has been, and probably always will be. But those who make the effort to climb the steep steps from Waterloo Place to the heights of what tends to be pushed aside as Edinburgh's Folly, will be surprised at the snippets of history which are there for the looking. There is the added advantage that Calton Hill is *never* as smothered in visitors as the Acropolis!

Napoleonic War Memorial

LOTHIAN CASTLES

It is often said that every man's home is his castle, and this would seem to be particularly true in Scotland, for nowhere else in Britain can there be found such a preponderance of castles, ruined or otherwise.

Merchiston Castle

But the name 'castle' is generally a misnomer in that, apart from the great strongholds of such cities as Edinburgh and Stirling, most of the so-called castles are in fact fortified mansions and towers, extended and added to over the years until the original nucleus of the building has almost disappeared under a defensive shell.

The tower house, or fortalice (which the dictionary tells us is simply a 'small fort') tends to be peculiar to Scotland and dates from the fifteenth to early seventeenth centuries. This was an era of great unrest when, during the Reformation, church lands were being carved up and redistributed in smaller chunks, each with its own laird's house which was required to be fortified by a Scots royal decree. This was probably just as well, since peace between the various warring factions was still some years away.

For obvious reasons, these stone-built mini-castles were strategically placed on high ground. Tall and gaunt, often parapetted and usually small-windowed, they sometimes had a curtain wall surround behind which livestock and local peasantry could be sheltered in times of strife.

The south of Scotland from the Forth to the Borders is a happy hunting ground for those interested in absorbing the heritage and tradition which seeps from these old stones, and many such buildings are featured elsewhere in this book. But a word of warning. An enticing ruin or old house surrounded by trees which may be spotted from the roadside could still be privately owned or occupied, so it is advisable to enquire locally as to its accessibility before marching up to the front door.

Joining the seemingly unending stream of houses boasting 'Queen Mary stayed here' is Bavelaw Castle, to be found among woodlands on the north slopes of the Pentland Hills about two miles south of Balerno.

The house rises to three storeys plus an attic. The ground-level entrance, defended by four gun-loops, leads into the well of the turnpike stair in the centre of the east side of the building. The ground floor, which is vaulted, is the old kitchen with its typically wide arched fireplace, and leading off it is the later addition of a small pantry.

Liberton Tower

The vaulted chambers in the north section are all at lower levels, which seems to point to it having been the original tower, maybe dating from the sixteenth century. It was in this section that Queen Mary was supposed to have had her pine-panelled room, no doubt also using the adjacent Hall with its ornamental plaster ceiling.

The small circular tower projecting at one corner of the building has no stair, and the

Craigmillar Castle

tiny pierced chambers in it – presumably built to provide defensive cover – are reached from the main rooms on each floor.

Sheltering among the Pentlands trees is Bonaly Tower, in Sturdy contrast to the nearby modern housing.

Perched high on the fringe of the Braid Hills, Liberton Tower has stared over the city and far out into the estuary since the fifteenth century. It is four storeys high with walls so thick that they accommodated three winding staircases. You have to look to the first floor for the front door, where you can spot the protruding stones which would have acted as anchor-points for a timber staircase which could be removed in times of attack. To complete the impression of solidity, the roof is of heavy stone flagging within a plain parapet walk drained by projecting spouts.

A prosperous merchant, Provost William Little, bought the tower in 1587, but one can only assume that he found his draughty dwelling not conducive to comfortable living, for in 1605 he built himself a more elegant modern mansion nearby – fortunately without knocking the old one down.

Liberton House, as the new home was called, was built on the normal L-plan of the era. There are three storeys in the main block and four in the wing, with a circular stair-tower in the angle topped by a tiny watch tower. Provost Little was obviously a cautious man, for the windows remained small and irregular, while gun-loops are judiciously scattered here and there. Both these buildings, more or less side by side, can be seen easily from the road.

Of all the fortified houses near Edinburgh, Craigmillar Castle takes precedence for its sheer grandeur, its size, and its importance as an outstanding example of medieval military architecture. This was no mere merchant's home, but a large baronial residence systematically enlarged and improved upon over three centuries in both domestic and defensive aspects.

As expected, the nucleus of the castle is the massive fourteenth-century L-shaped tower sitting on the southern edge of a 30-foot high rock, which falls away in a steep cliff from the tower's base. The Great Hall occupies the first floor, and to give some idea of the size of this tower, the hall alone measures 30 feet by nearly 21 feet, and is 25 feet high, with a large hooded fireplace at one end.

Curtain walls were the first addition to the tower, built flush with the natural cliff on one side, but on the other sides extending to form a courtyard, with round towers at the four corners. The tower facing the main castle approach must be one of the earliest batteries in Scotland, as it is amply provided with openings for cannon.

Later, domestic quarters appear to have been erected within the courtyard, comprising cellars, kitchen, and garret bedrooms. There were also a well-house and bakery and, to complete the picture, a dungeon – in which a human skeleton was found in 1813! Some time around the mid-sixteenth century, a second wall was erected to form an outer courtyard, incorporating a round tower said to be a dovecot. But as the roosting holes took the form of gun-loops, strange birds must have been housed here.

St Mary's Cathedral

Cruciform in plan, St Mary's is a huge church 263 feet long, with a central spire 275 feet high. The two smaller spires at the west end were additions during the First World War, and are named the Barbara and Mary Spires after the two sisters whose benevolence enabled the founding of the cathedral.

Inside, the white marble sculpture of the screen behind the High Altar is flanked by two statues: St Margaret of Scotland, and St Columba to represent the European and Celtic influences in the Scottish church. The choirstalls of walnut, beautifully carved, are a fine example of Victorian craftsmanship, as are the wrought iron screens, made in Coventry in 1880 and in medieval colouring. The pulpit, of Caen stone, has marble pillars in the Italian style; the carved figures represent Christ, St Peter, John the Baptist, and the four evangelists.

The main fabric of the cathedral was completed in 1879. Inflation was then a problem as it is today, and any further building work was temporarily halted for some years until more money could be raised. The Lady Chapel was added in 1898, and it is here where the weekday morning services are held. The Chapel of Resurrection is also part of the cathedral war memorial, and contains some interesting ancient flags.

During the seventeenth century, the lands surrounding where the cathedral now stands belonged to families living in the Royal Mile, who

Surmounted by three magnificent spires, the vast bulk of St Mary's Episcopal Cathedral in Palmerston Place dominates much of the West End's professional belt with its modernised Georgian offices. The cathedral's architecture, its intricate carved stonework, and its very size combine to give a first impression of greater age than it can claim, as building did not even start until 1874.

Although the Diocese of Edinburgh was founded in 1633 by Charles I, it was without a cathedral for more than 150 years after disestablishment in 1689. In the mid-1800s, however, the Misses Barbara and Mary Walker conceived the idea of building and partly endowing a cathedral for the diocese, using their own land as the site. The architect was selected by competition, and the task fell to Sir George Gilbert Scott, who was well-experienced in restoring medieval Gothic churches, and who drew his inspiration from the remaining Scottish cathedrals of that era.

built their country houses here. Old maps show several mansion houses set in parkland with a lake. One of these houses was Easter Coates House and in 1813 it came into the possession of the Walker family.

The original house, considerably added to in the last century, was L-shaped with a small stair-wing projecting to the west of the main block. Only two storeys and an attic high, it has two large angle-turrets, containing little chambers, overhanging the south gable. Built in 1615 by Sir John Byres, an Edinburgh merchant, it is the oldest building still surviving intact in the New Town.

When the estate passed to the Walker family in 1813, restoration work included the incorporation into the stonework of two door lintels, dated 1600 and 1601, together with some pieces of sculpture believed to have come from a demolished mansion in the Cowgate which had been traditionally known as the residence of the French Embassy in Queen Mary's time.

The choral service held at the cathedral every day since its opening was made possible by the foundation of a Choir School housed in the Old Manor House of Easter Coates. Additional buildings were erected to accommodate more boys, and a Song School was provided in 1887. The Choir School, the only one in Scotland, continued the tradition of the *Sang Schules* which

produced much Scottish medieval music. In 1971 came the decision to develop it into a school for musically-gifted children; now called St Mary's Music School, it is well-known as a residential school for outstandingly talented children from all over the country.

One of the cathedral's most valued possessions is a painting hanging in the north choir aisle. Called 'The Presence', it was painted in the cathedral by the late Capt A. E. Borthwick in 1910. Soon after it was completed, the picture was exhibited throughout the UK before being sent to Germany for reproductions to be made. It was still in Munich when the First World War broke out, and it was sold to an American firm for £5000 instead of being returned to its owner.

It disappeared for some time until a portion of the picture was used by a New York newspaper to illustrate an article, an illustration that was to involve the paper in legal action for breach of copyright.

After the war, Congress passed a special Act to enable the picture to be returned to Scotland instead of being sold as confiscated enemy property. The painting was preserved in the vaults of the Royal Scottish Academy during the Second World War until, in December 1944, Capt Borthwick and his wife presented it to the cathedral – the church in which they had been married.

EDINBURGH MUSEUMS

Edinburgh's main museum of local history is Huntly House. Its displays range through Roman artefacts found during nearby archaeological digs, historic documents and prints, the wooden pipes which brought the city's first water supply, exquisite silverware, reconstructions of traditional industries, and period rooms peopled by extraordinarily life-like models – including the occasional mouse!

These treasures from the capital's past could have no more suitable resting-place, for Huntly House, attractive and intimate with its many small connecting rooms, was in existence long before many of its exhibits had ever been dreamed about.

The land in the Royal Mile was acquired and the house built by James Aitchison (or

Inside Huntly House Museum

Acheson) in 1517. Suffering badly during the English invasion of 1544 when it was almost reduced to rubble, re-building in 1570 introduced a new frontage which extended the property ten feet into the street.

In 1647, Huntly House was taken over by the Incorporation (or Union) of Hammermen, the metal workers of the Canongate, as a meeting place for the craftsmen and a suitable investment for their funds. A convening house was built, and the hammermen secured their future finances by renting out the remaining accommodation. Some years later, they built an extension to the south, working on the logical theory of more tenants, more money.

The property was retained by the hammermen until 1762, by which time it housed 16 tenants representing a considerable cross-section of the community, including a peer, weavers, a plumber, a gardener, and a painter.

In the 1880s, Huntly House went the way of so much Royal Mile property after the spread to the New Town. Neglect and decay set in, and the house was partitioned off into small dwellings, inhabited only by the poorer people living in squalid conditions. Eventually becoming unfit for habitation, the house was acquired by Edinburgh Corporation in 1924. Under the guidance of architect Sir Frank Mears, an ambitious restoration programme was undertaken, and eight years later Huntly House was opened as the principal city museum.

A former tavern adjoining the house at the entrance to Bakehouse Close was taken over in 1969, and is now the main entrance and reception area for the museum. Bakehouse Close, also now restored and giving a tantalising glimpse of Salisbury Crags beyond, was the eighteenth-century headquarters of the Incorporation of the Bakers of Canongate.

One of the 'Speaking Panels' at Huntly House

The model figures of a pompous town crier and his strutting drummer boy outside Huntly House serve to remind visitors of its other name, The Speaking House, a phrase coined by historian Robert Chambers in 1823 when referring to the four panels of Latin

Main Hall of the Royal
Museum of Scotland

Huntly House Museum:
Open:
Monday–Saturday:
10.00 am–5.00 pm
(June–September:
10.00 am–6.00 pm)
During the Edinburgh
Festival, Sundays:
2.00 pm–5.00 pm

For general information
on Royal Museums,
telephone: 031–225
7534

The red sandstone building at the east end of Queen Street, designed in 1885 by Rowand Anderson, is sometimes likened to the Doge's Palace in Venice, although the exterior decoration stops far short of the mural paintings which grace that magnificent facade. It houses a most comprehensive collection of Scottish history and everyday life from the Stone Age to the present. Archaeology has played a big part in its tradition, the first donation to this museum being prehistoric relics uncovered at nearby Duddingston, where lake-dwellers were believed to have been the original settlers.

The most striking features of the Chambers Street museum are its lofty main hall of glass and elegant Victorian cast iron galleries, created by Francis Fowkes in 1861. The scope of the museum is worldwide rather than domestic, for its collections cover the decorative arts, natural history and geology of the whole world, following on logically to technology and space age exhibits.

Certain specialist collections also come under the auspices of the new organisation, the result of the National Heritage (Scotland) Act.

Situated appropriately within the Royal Highland Showground at Ingliston is the agricultural museum, built in the late 1970s. During the summer months this houses exhibitions devoted to various aspects of farming, Scotland's major industry.

At East Fortune, roads may have to be closed and fences moved when some of the larger exhibits arrive – this East Lothian war-time airstrip is the site of the Museum of Flight, which has an ever-growing collection of aircraft large and small.

High on Edinburgh Castle rock near the National War Memorial is the Scottish United Services Museum. Comprising several rooms, the exhibits are arranged to cover the different branches of the armed services, forming a display of the uniforms, equipment and weapons used during centuries of strife.

Other museums within the group are Shambellie House Museum of Costume near Dumfries, and Biggar Gasworks Museum in Lanarkshire.

mottoes inset on the 1570 frontage. Translated, they read:

> *Today for me, tomorrow for thee, why therefore carest thou?*
>
> *As thou art master of thy tongue, so also am I master of my ears.*
>
> *The affair of mortals to a steadfast mind is as a shadow.*
>
> *There is hope of another life.*

The last was proved prophetic, and a fifth panel added on the opening of the museum in 1932 reads, appropriately enough:

> *I am old, but renew my youth.*

Millions of objects gathered over more than 200 years have been brought together in Scotland's national museums to form an outstanding collection of treasures spanning the centuries from the simple tools of prehistory to the latest in electronic genius.

Reorganisation in October 1985 brought the museums under one board of trustees, but although they now function under the umbrella of the National Museums of Scotland, each has remained in its former location and retains the specialised features for which each has become known.

Display at Scottish Agricultural Museum

SCOTMID COACH COLLECTION

It is hoped to be able to open the collection to the public when more suitable premises are found; at the time of going to print visits may be made by appointment through Mr T. McKnight, telephone 031-229 2424. City tours by horse and carriage may also be booked; and the coaches are available for wedding hire.

A diesel van having its paintwork touched up looks distinctly out of place alongside the elegant lines of a landau, a barouche, or a more chunky hansom cab, but such contrasts are quite commonplace at the paint workshops of the Scotmid Co-operative Society in Edinburgh, more familiarly known by its pre-merger name of St Cuthbert's. Few local residents realise that the society's headquarters in Edinburgh house a unique private collection of some 25 Victorian horse-drawn carriages restored to full roadworthy standards. Probably even fewer people are aware that the society holds the coveted position of Coachpainters to the Queen by Royal Appointment, ceremonial vehicles being sent here from the Royal Mews in London for regular refurbishing.

For many years now, the society has been quietly rescuing discarded nineteenth-century transport – including two rather battered coaches which were found half-buried in a coal store – and through the expertise of wheelwrights, joiners, saddlers and an up-holsterer, restoring them to their former glory.

Some idea of the work which goes into such restoration can be appreciated when one discovers that the vehicles are not given just a quick repaint; they receive ten coats of paint followed by ten coats of varnish, plus freehand decoration, to produce a hard mirror-like finish. And what may appear to be painted wheel guards are more likely to be hand-stitched patent leather.

The restored carriages of the collection cover most modes of Victorian transport, and include a stagecoach which needed four horses to pull it; an 1824 fire engine with a manual water pump; an 1830 station brake; a sombre black hearse with silver fittings and intricately engraved glass sides; a fourteen-seater brake; a little Victoria, the horse-drawn bath chair which supposedly got its name from transporting Queen Victoria round the estate when she stayed at Balmoral; and a butcher's van used by the society until relatively recently.

The open convertible coaches are frequently used by the Royal Family on such occasions as Ascot. The carriage which took Lady Diana to her wedding, and then carried the newly-weds on the first stage of their honeymoon, came from the society.

Probably the society's most spectacular ceremonial triumph was on June 23rd, 1953, when it provided thirteen carriages and thirteen pairs of horses for the procession marking the Queen's first visit to Edinburgh after her coronation. The Crown Jewels were brought out of the Castle's safekeeping for the first time in 300 years for the Scottish ceremony.

One cannot ignore the horses which for so many years were part of the city scene on the milk deliveries. Over the years, St Cuthbert's supplied horses from its stud to the Royal Family and various police forces, but the most famous graduate of the stables was Cicero. Spotted on his milk round during a royal visit to the capital after the war, Cicero was recruited into the Household Cavalry and went on to become its longest-serving drum horse.

By the time the dairy closed, the society's horse-force was down to twelve animals, and eight were found new homes, chosen from the hundreds of offers which flooded in. Trigger, Ranger, Micky and Billy, all heavy hunter class horses, happily adapted to their new roles, helping to bring a reminder of past elegance to the streets of Edinburgh.

ART GALLERIES

In 1984, the Scottish Gallery of Modern Art took up residence in its new permanent home, an elegant neo-classical nineteenth-century building in Belford Road. Its ever-expanding 24-year-old collection, the most comprehensive of its kind outside the Tate, had completely outgrown the former gallery at Inverleith House in the Botanic Gardens, but the new premises are ideal. Thankfully, the conversion of the former school has provided the gallery with a green and open setting, without traffic thundering past its front door. With 12 acres of land to play with, the gallery now has ample scope to display the modernistic sculptures which, before, were somewhat regimented into a small section of Inverleith's back lawn. The building houses a mix of galleries large and small to accommodate the works of twentieth-century artists who have expressed themselves in various media on a huge diversity of themes.

There is a library of books, periodicals and catalogues on twentieth-century art, and a study collection of prints and drawings is available to visitors by arrangement. Also housed here is the conservation department serving the National Galleries of Scotland. The gallery has its own shop, and an extremely pleasant restaurant is situated on the lower ground floor.

Francois Boucher's *Madame de Pompadour* at the National Gallery of Scotland

The National Gallery of Scotland on The Mound holds the finest small collection of paintings in Europe, if not in the world. A carefully selected group of masterpieces dating from about 1400 to 1900 is housed in the building, a neo-classical structure by architect William Playfair.

Among the finest oils are those lent by the Duke of Sutherland, including five Titians, three Raphaels, three Rembrandts, and nine Poussins. And no visit would be complete without seeing the two moving panels, formerly in Edinburgh's Trinity Church, by Hugo van der Goes, presently on loan from the Queen.

As a contrast to the old masters there is the fresh appeal of French nineteenth-century art – a rare flower piece by Delacroix, Cezanne's 'La Monagne Sainte Victoire', Monet's 'Poplars on the Epte', and Degas' 'Diego Martelli'.

Scottish painting is represented by the works of Ramsay, Raeburn, and Wilkie, as well as a feast of immaculately executed fairy pictures by Joseph Noel Paton. The Gallery also houses a vast collection of some 19,000 prints, drawings and watercolours, including the famous Vaughan Bequest of Turner watercolours.

The Scottish National Portrait Gallery in Queen Street adds a whole new dimension to an understanding of Scotland's colourful and dramatic history. Here you can come face to face with great Scots from the sixteenth century to the present day, many of them people whose influence spread far beyond Scotland as scientists, writers, explorers, artists, and statesmen.

Mary Queen of Scots, the romantic Jacobites, philosopher David Hume, Robert Burns, Sir Walter Scott, Ramsay MacDonald and Hugh MacDiarmid are among the faces which line the walls of their Gothic revival home. Many of the portraits are great works of art in their own right by artists such as Lely, Batoni, Ramsay, Reynolds, Gainsborough, Raeburn, Rodin, Epstein and Kokoschka.

The Portrait Gallery is not all in the past, however, but keeps pace with the times: a collection of recently commissioned portraits of famous contemporary figures is now being built up, and includes one of the Queen Mother.

This gallery also holds an outstanding collection of Scottish photography, including 5,000 works by the pioneers Hill and Adamson. The collection was further enlarged in late 1985 by Sir Alan Muir Wood, who gifted the 900 prints and negatives taken by and given to his ancestor John Muir Wood in the 1840s.

The City of Edinburgh has its own City Arts Centre in Market Street. Formerly a substantial late-Victorian warehouse, the premises have been transformed into an imposing arts centre, housing the city's permanent collection of Scottish paintings, drawings, prints and sculpture. Throughout the year, temporary exhibitions of fine art and decorative art are on display.

Facing Princes Street at the foot of The Mound, and surmounted by Steell's statue of Queen Victoria perched above its graceful columns, is the Royal Scottish Academy which regularly holds exhibitions featuring the work of its members.

THE ROYAL OBSERVATORY

The Royal Observatory, set high above the city on Blackford Hill, is a familiar Edinburgh landmark, but few people know what goes on under its great copper dome, or realise that it plays a major role in the worldwide science of probing deeper and ever deeper into the mysteries of the great galaxies of which Earth is only a miniscule part.

Forming part of the Science and Engineering Research Council of the United Kingdom, the observatory is responsible for providing and running facilities for UK astronomers, and supporting research in the universities. A major part of its activity is directed to the development and operation of a number of telescopes and associated equipment scattered round the globe, including the UK 1.2 metre Schmidt Telescope sited in Australia, the high-speed measuring machine in Edinburgh, and both the UK 3.8

metre infrared telescope and the UK/Netherlands millimetre telescope sited near the summit of Mauna Kea, an extinct volcano in Hawaii, at an altitude of over 4000 metres.

As well as the operation of these facilities, the observatory has an active research group, advanced electronic and mechanical workshops, photographic laboratories, an extensive library, and powerful computing facilities directly linked with other major computing centres in Britain and overseas.

The UK 1.2 metre Schmidt Telescope, described as the most powerful camera in the world, is located on Siding Spring Mountain in New South Wales, Australia, in order to take advantage of the dark, clear skies characteristic of the region. Originally its prime purpose was to assist in compiling an atlas of the southern skies, capturing star images far fainter than had previously been recorded. Its field of view covers an area more than 180 times the area of the disc of the full moon, this wide angle enabling the telescope to record more than a million stars on a single photograph.

This superb instrument has now taken more than 10,000 photographs for thousands of researchers at hundreds of institutions in dozens of countries. In addition some 200 copies of the sky atlas, which probes deeper than any comparable survey, have been distributed throughout the world. Objects studied range from nearby members of the Solar System such as comets and minor planets, to the distant and mysterious quasars near the edge of the observable universe, which have been investigated to assist research into the formation of stars and galaxies, and the shape and dynamics of gaseous nebulae.

The high-speed automatic COSMOS measuring machine can detect and measure the images which are typically recorded on a Schmidt photographic plate. It does this with incredible precision, locating objects on the photograph to within one-thousandth of a millimetre, and taking only three hours to extract the details of a million stars – a task which, it is calculated, would take seven years if attempted manually.

Although designed for astronomical research, and vital for studying the large-scale distribution of matter in the universe, COSMOS (an acronym derived from Co-Ordinates, Sizes, Magnitudes, Orientations, Shapes) has contributed to other branches of science, such as medicine, aerial photography, radar analysis, and geology, proving invaluable wherever image analysis is required.

With ever-improving telescopes and instrumentation, astronomers can observe deeper into space than ever before, looking thousands of millions of light years distant. To handle the increasing amount of information

The 3.8 UK Infrared Telescope (UKIRT), the largest in the world specifically designed for observations at infrared wavelengths is located on the 4200m summit of Mauna Kea Hawaii. It is operated by staff of the Royal Observatory

becoming available, powerful and fast computing facilities are of prime importance.

The Royal Observatory has four large computer systems, a British GEC 4090 and three VAX 11 devices, one of which is part of the Starlink Network connecting major observatories and universities throughout Britain, ensuring compatibility of programmes and avoiding duplication of work at different establishments.

Among the increasing number of large telescopes on Mauna Kea in Hawaii is the UK Infrared Telescope, operated and maintained by the staff of the Royal Observatory on overseas duty tour. Opened in 1979, the telescope collects and measures the tiny amounts of infrared or heat radiation coming from objects in space. To achieve this, the telescope is situated in one of the clearest, driest places in the world, free of cloud and water vapour, both of which absorb infrared radiation.

The telescope mirror, 3.8 metres in diameter, is much thinner than usual for an instrument of this size, thanks to ingenious design, and enables astronomers to undertake a wide range of observation programmes. For example, it was the first instrument to detect infrared radiation emitted by Halley's Comet. To measure such tiny amounts of radiation, the telescope detectors must be kept extremely cold, working at temperatures close to absolute zero. Much of the advanced design and manufacture of such sophisticated equipment is the responsibility of the Technology Unit at the Royal Observatory.

Since first becoming involved in studying the sky from rockets and satellites in the 1960s, the observatory is now involved in the operation of the Hubble Space Telescope launched by the Space Shuttle into low earth orbit. The extreme sensitivity of this space telescope opens up prospects of major advances in all fields of astronomical research and discovery. Unit staff are also designing a camera for the Infrared Space Observatory due for launch in the 1990s.

The library at the observatory is believed to be the most complete collection of its sort in the world. Containing thousands of textbooks and standard works on all aspects of astronomy, the library provides information ranging from ancient texts to the most recent observational reports. At its core is the Crawford Collection of historical, astronomical and mathematical works dating from the thirteenth to the late nineteenth centuries.

The visitor centre is open throughout the year, providing the public with an opportunity to learn some basic principles and to study the work done at the observatory. A wide range of displays is included, with many spectacular celestial photographs on view. A number of telescopes are also available for public observing on clear nights from September to March, and arrangements can be made for group visits.

This article was kindly contributed exclusively for Explore Edinburgh *by Mr Russell D. Eberst, Information Officer at the Royal Observatory, Edinburgh.*

Astronomers at the Observatory examine an infrared spectrum of the star HR 8824 obtained from Mauna Kea, Hawaii

DUDDINGSTON

Duddingston is a quiet, almost rural, village sheltering under the south-eastern slopes of Arthur's Seat, with a wealth of heritage background almost out of proportion to its size.

Lake-dwellers living in primitive huts built on stilts were the first people to settle on the shores of Duddingston Loch, which centuries later was to yield up weapons and jewellery attributed to the Bronze Age. The settlement became permanent, and after King David I had gifted the lands to the Abbot of Kelso in the 1100s, his monks built the church overlooking the loch. Basically Norman in style, there have been many changes both inside and out although many of its original features remain, such as the Lepers' Squint overlooking the chancel. This was probably made to accommodate worshippers from the leper colony at nearby Liberton.

Standing by the churchyard gate is the six-sided watchtower built in the 1800s, where two unfortunate elders of the church had to spend their nights on guard for three weeks after an interment to deter any hopeful body-snatchers. An interesting building in itself, it is now used as the Session House and vestry for the church.

Also at the gate are two more reminders of the past. The loupin'-on stane was for the benefit of sedate ladies or elderly and over-fat gentlemen mounting and dismounting from their horses. Nearby is the jougs' collar, an iron hoop chained to the wall into which nagging wives were locked and left to the ridicule of the rest of the village.

Perched on the loch-side at the bottom of the Manse garden is a two-storey octagonal tower with its own true tale. The Reverend John Thomson, minister of Duddingston from 1805 until 1840, was probably better known in his capacity as a landscape painter. Christening the tower Edinburgh, he used the top storey as his studio when escaping from parochial duties, leaving messages for uninvited guests that he had 'gone to Edinburgh'. So honour was upheld with truth, and some of his many paintings now hang in the city's art galleries.

The Sheep Heid Inn, to be found off Old Church Lane in The Causeway, has the distinction of being Scotland's oldest licensed premises. Built in 1360 as a hostelry – and incidentally much used before and after Sunday service at the kirk, the excuse being that the horses were stabled there – its original exterior remains unchanged, and the internal alterations over the years have done nothing to destroy its old quaintness and charm. Still in use today is the skittle alley, where Mary Queen of Scots is reputed to have enjoyed the occasional game of bowls when staying at Craigmillar Castle.

A large picture on the bar wall, depicting preparations for the Battle of Prestonpans on the morning of 21 September 1745, reminds today's customers that Bonnie Prince Charlie visited the pub before the famous confrontation.

Whether he slept in Duddingston or not is debatable – some records have him spending the night before the battle at Holyroodhouse. Certainly, a red-tiled restored house in The Causeway, once another tavern, bears a stone plaque above the door which reads: 'In this house, 19 September 1745, Prince Charles Edward Stuart held his Council of War before the Battle of Prestonpans'.

But wherever he may or may not have stayed, he obviously slept well, for that battle was a resounding victory for Prince Charles and his men, which they celebrated by hauling the English General Cope's huge stagecoach all the way back to Duddingston before sharing out the spoils of war at their encampment near the village.

The painter parson's studio retreat 'Edinburgh'

Neidpath Castle by the river Tweed

Melrose Abbey

HERMITAGE OF BRAID

For further information:
Telephone
031 447 7145, or contact
Edinburgh District Council
Recreation Department

Tucked under the hills between Liberton and Morningside, the park of the Hermitage of Braid forms an area of unspoilt countryside frequently forgotten, although well within the city itself. The Braid Burn flows through the wooded gorge where trees meet overhead, while a fairly gentle slope leads up to the summit of Blackford Hill with its fine views.

A network of tracks, trails and paths reveals a number of unexpected features in this little oasis, not the least of which is Hermitage House itself, now the visitor and information centre. It was built in 1785 for Charles Gordon of Cluny by a local builder in the style of Adam, hence its rather unkind pseudonym 'carpenters' Gothic'.

The Hermitage of Braid

Blackford Pond

A later addition to the estate was the gatehouse in Braid Road. Formerly the old Morningside Tollhouse, it was demolished on its original site after the abolition of toll roads, and rebuilt as the Hermitage lodge in the 1880s.

Near the waterfall where the burn runs alongside the main drive is the site of a corn mill, later used for papermaking until the late 1700s. A little further on, a track leads to the walled garden and a doocot (dovecot) containing almost 2,000 nesting boxes, which dates from the seventeenth or early eighteenth century. Set into the south bank near the house is the old ice house, where ice collected from ponds in winter would have been stored until needed for cooling and preserving food and drink the following summer.

From the stable block a woodland trail borders the gorge, which is over 30 yards deep in places, and crossing the bridge will take you back to the walled garden, set in the area where once Braid Castle stood.

Approaching the park from Cluny Gardens, you come first to Blackford Pond, populated by numerous tame ducks well fed by the local children, and once the home of the nineteenth-century Waverley Curling Club. Corbie's Crag, higher up and populated this time by crows, leads on through Blackford Glen towards the summit of Blackford Hill.

The visitor centre in the house incorporates information displays and exhibitions, a day centre for school groups, and also serves as a base for the Countryside Ranger Service, responsible for protection of the area and closely associated with the activities of the Hermitage Conservation Group.

The job of the Scottish Countryside Rangers' Association is to provide information on their particular area, and to promote an understanding of how the countryside has evolved, and how the many people who work in it – farmer, landowner, forester, industrialist – interrelate. At visitor centres such as that at Hermitage of Braid there are displays of local interest, and the Rangers can supply details of various activities available such as sports, or less strenuous rambling and bird-watching trips.

In addition to helping the public, the Rangers' aim is to protect the countryside, and assist in its conservation. There are more than 120 Rangers in Scotland, working in country parks, private estates, and in conjunction with local authorities and other bodies such as the National Trust and the Scottish Wildlife Trust.

SONS OF EDINBURGH

Painters, scientists, poets, lawyers – the list is almost endless – these are the Sons of Edinburgh whose efforts for the benefit of mankind, our heritage and culture are famous far beyond the city limits. Some were of humble origins, others were endowed with more worldly advantages, but all achieved the distinction of becoming household names not only during their lifetime, but for all time.

Scottish writers made a considerable impact in the field of literature, the quality of their output rivalled only by its sheer volume. The good citizens of Ayrshire are not likely to allow anyone to forget the works of their prodigious poet, Robert Burns; in the east, the people of Edinburgh are staunch supporters of Sir Walter Scott and Robert Louis Stevenson. Much of their fascination stems from the knowledge that their books are largely based on or around places and localities which still exist today.

Walter Scott, who was educated at Edinburgh High School and studied law at the University, was called to the Bar in 1792. Already dabbling in writing, his pleasure in the rolling countryside to the south prompted the publishing of *Border Minstrelsy* and *The Lay of the Last Minstrel*, after which Scott took up a partnership in Ballantyne's printing business in 1805. The company's eventual collapse 20 years later was attributed largely to Scott's own extravagances, and he spent the rest of his life trying to pay off the enormous debts.

Apart from producing a stream of masterpieces – the *Waverley* novels, *Rob Roy*, the *Heart of Midlothian*, *Guy Mannering*, *Bride of Lammermoor* and many others, some of which he wrote at his Borders home of Abbotsford – Scott still managed to devote considerable time and energy to the affairs of his home town. He was instrumental in the return to Edinburgh of the cannon Mons Meg, which he rightly believed belonged to the city and not to London; he was largely responsible for stage-managing the visit of George IV to the capital in 1822; he was one of the founders of Edinburgh Academy.

Edinburgh's other prolific writer was, of course, Robert Louis Stevenson. One of his achievements while studying engineering at the university was to win a silver medal for a paper on the unlikely subject of lighthouse improvements! He abandoned engineering in favour of law, graduated in 1875, but never practised.

Already set on a literary path, Stevenson achieved instant acclaim with his book *Treasure Island*. This was followed by the success – or notoriety – of *Dr Jekyll and Mr Hyde*, based on the doings of the real-life Deacon Brodie. This was the pattern he chose to follow, using real people as models for his characters, and real places for the locations. So we find South Queensferry and Corstorphine as settings for *Kidnapped*; Cramond for *House of Shaw*; Yellowcraigs for *Treasure Island*; and his own summer retreat of Swanston Cottage for *St Ives*.

Having suffered from chest trouble since a child, and regarding Edinburgh as having a climate which was 'one of the vilest under heaven', Stevenson restlessly travelled Europe, America and the Pacific islands in a bid for relief. Settling in Samoa in 1890, there was just time for him to write *Catriona* as the sequel to *Kidnapped* before he died from a brain haemorrhage in 1894. His grave is on the South Pacific island, but he is remembered in Edinburgh by a memorial bronze in St Giles.

A certain medical graduate who obviously had his mind on other things was Arthur Conan Doyle. In 1891, he submitted a series of short stories to The Strand Magazine entitled *The Adventures of Sherlock Holmes*. They attracted so much interest that he turned his hand to full-length books which today are as popular as ever, both in print and on the small screen. Sir Arthur returned to his original profession during the South African War when he served as a physician between 1899 and 1902.

Other medical men of Edinburgh made contributions to their profession for which we should all be thankful. Chloroform was introduced by baker's son Sir James Simpson in 1847, a few years after his appointment as Professor of Midwifery at Edinburgh University.

Surgery underwent a complete revolution when Joseph Lister discovered antiseptics. Later Lord Lister, he studied the methods used by the celebrated surgeon, James Syme, in the 1850s, and continued his research – greatly influenced by the work of Louis Pasteur – during the twelve years he spent as Professor of Clinical

Abbotsford, home of Sir Walter Scott

Surgery at Edinburgh University, while also practising at the Royal Infirmary.

It is said that John Napier spent hours pacing the roof walk of his home at Merchiston Castle puzzling out his many inventions. It is certain that generations of schoolchildren have spent even more hours puzzling over his most devious of ideas – the dreaded logarithms. Originally they were called artificial numbers, and Napier used to explain his theories by the use of little rods, which came to be known as Napier's Bones, and later juggling with the metal plates of what must have been a forerunner of today's calculating machine.

John Napier was obviously of an enquiring mind. In addition to these brain-twisters, he also experimented with the alternative uses of manure; invented the present notation of decimal fractions; and invented a hydraulic screw for clearing water out of coal mines, for which he was granted a monopoly. It is appropriate that the centuries-old Merchiston Castle where he lived has now been incorporated into the modern college which bears his name.

Edinburgh has produced its share of artists. Father and son Alexander and Patrick Nasmyth were both portrait and landscape painters of note, but it was their contemporary Sir Henry Raeburn whose works earned him the accolade of 'the Scottish Reynolds'.

Son of an Edinburgh manufacturer, Raeburn started his career at the age of 16 when he began painting watercolour miniatures of his friends. In 1778, he was fortunate (or prudent) enough to marry a widow of means, and on the advice of Reynolds he went to Rome to study painting. Returning to Edinburgh ten years later, he was for 30 years a fashionable portrait painter. During these years, he painted all his contemporaries of note except, we are told, Burns. Although some of his works hang in the city's galleries, most of his paintings are to be found chiefly in Scotland's private mansions.

Francis Jeffrey, Lord Jeffrey the judge and critic, was one of the founders of the controversial Edinburgh Review, a magazine well-known for its outspoken opinions and criticisms. Educated at the High School and University, Lord Jeffrey was admitted to the Scottish Bar in 1794, but for some years could obtain little work as a barrister owing to his extreme Whig views. While editor of the Review, and doubtless taking the opportunity to air some of those views, he was at one stage challenged to a duel over remarks made in an article. However, both contestants were arrested before the fight could take place – and thereafter became firm friends.

Scots are quick to allow Alexander Graham Bell back into the fold when the telephone is mentioned, despite the fact that he emigrated to Canada and then America before the new-fangled instrument was really under way. The first basic telephone was made in Boston, and Bell introduced a more sophisticated model to England and France in 1877. A less well-known aspect of his life was a deep involvement in education for the deaf.

When the paper poppies bloom in November each year, they form annual tribute not only to the ordinary men who lost their lives in the First World War, but also to the man who led the British troops to victory, Field-Marshal Earl Haig, who was born in Edinburgh's Charlotte Square in 1861, and educated at Oxford and Sandhurst. The young Douglas Haig rose rapidly in his chosen career. He became Commander-in-Chief of the British Forces during the First World War. Created an earl in 1919, when he was Commander-in-Chief of Home Forces, Field-Marshal Haig devoted his retirement to the well-being of ex-servicemen, becoming president of the newly-formed British Legion and chairman of the United Services Fund.

THE PENTLAND HILLS

For further information:
Countryside Information
Centre,
Hillend Park, Edinburgh
Tel. 031-445-3383

Castlelaw Fort

How to get there:
Take the A702 Biggar
road from Hillend; after 2
miles the fort is clearly
signposted up a minor
road into the Pentlands

Car parking: Free

Warning: When the red
flags are flying, signifying
gunnery practice on the
army's nearby range, do
not stray from the fort area

S cald Law, Cauldstane Slap, Caerketton, Threipmuir may sound a weird mouthful to a stranger, but to the native of Edinburgh such names conjure up the picture of the rounded peaks of the Pentland Hills, the first glimpse of which prompts many a returning traveller to comment 'nearly home'.

C overing more than 80 square miles, the thin wedge of the Pentland Hills stretches for 16 miles from the city's south-west corner to Carnwath in Strathclyde. Throughout that length no road has ever been built to straddle the unspoiled beauty of valleys, peaks and streams, rather to the disgust of those who live on the southern slopes and have to go all the way round to get to Edinburgh!

T he geology of the range reveals much about the origins of the hills. They were once much higher than they are today, the younger, softer strata having eroded away to leave hard, mostly very old rocks, the oldest being Silurian formed about 400 million years ago. Fossilised remains of molluscs, corals and starfish have been found in this strata, clear evidence that when they were laid down the land was covered by a warm shallow sea. This rock is only seen in a few places, and resembles near-vertical layers of hardened grey-green mud.

F or a long time after the Silurian period, thousands of feet of rock were worn away leaving a platform on which sandstones and conglomerates were deposited, and while this was happening, volcanoes began erupting a few miles to the north. This was the upheaval which was to shape the Edinburgh landscape as we know it now, and huge lava-flows from these volcanoes covered the Pentlands time and time again, leaving behind the solidified lava and ash which make up a large part of the northern end of the hills. Following the eruptions, a tropical climate brought about the growth of tree-like ferns on the lower ground, ferns whose fossils now provide coal.

T he Ice Age was the last great geological event, when from about a million years ago, sheets of ice up to 3,000 feet thick worked their way from the western Highlands across the Pentlands, grinding off the sharp edges of rock and leaving the familiar rounded hills of today.

Although some believe the name of the range derives from Pictland, traces of prehistoric settlements are scarce apart from a series of mainly Iron Age forts on the eastern slopes, and hilltop cairns on Carnethy Hill and East Cairn Hill which are thought to have been used in connection with sun-worship. In the Middle Ages, West Linton was a centre for sheep and cattle trading, strategically placed on one of the drove roads between the Border country, central Scotland and the Highlands. Known as the Threver Road, this crossed the hills at Cauldstane Slap, best-known of the Pentland passes.

The enthusiastic walker may presume to think that the Pentlands were put there as a vast recreational playground. In fact, much of the area is privately-owned and devoted to farming. Beef and dairy cattle are kept on the lower slopes, while the hardy Blackface sheep nibble their way through the heather and tough grass of the uplands. Large areas have been assigned to agricultural research, and the army makes extensive use of the hills for its training programmes. Other uses include water catchment and storage in the 13 reservoirs scattered throughout the range which contribute four million gallons of pure water towards Edinburgh's daily consumption.

You cannot, therefore, assume that it is permissible to go wherever you want, and public use is restricted in some areas. Nevertheless, good rights-of-way do exist, providing nearly 60 miles of footpaths.

Before venturing into the hills, it would be a wise precaution for the novice to contact the Countryside Information Centre at Hillend Park, Edinburgh, where the ranger service is able to advise and assist, providing any necessary literature.

CASTLELAW FORT

Castlelaw Fort in the Pentlands is not the sort of place to visit on a dull November afternoon, especially on your own. Granted there's a farm a couple of hundred yards down the hill, and rifle shots ring out as the army practices knocking the heads off little cardboard men, but nevertheless the ghosts of the Iron Age people who once inhabited the fort seem very close as you intrude into their underground burrow. The odd sheep suddenly deciding to walk across the skylight just above your head is liable to do funny things to your blood pressure, and you may not stay long!

CASTLELAW FORT

You have to duck your head to enter; these prehistoric people must have been very small. The curved passage, which is about 70 feet long and little more than a yard wide, is lined with a wall of piled-up rocks and boulders only four or five feet high. A concrete roof now protects the site, completely grass-covered on the outside.

Leading off the passage is an obvious doorway of a single boulder lintel supported on two hefty stone uprights. It is almost a hands-and-knees exercise to get through, but one is rewarded by finding a circular chamber – now fortunately equipped with a skylight – which may have served as a dwelling, albeit a very little one, a storeroom or a workshop.

Dating from the last centuries BC, the settlement was defended by three ramparts and ditches, excavations showing that the original rampart with its timber palisade and ditch had been succeeded by two outer lines of defence. A souterrain, or earth house, had been constructed in one of the ditches. The fort was probably abandoned in Roman times.

SWANSTON

Thatched roofs are rare in Scotland, but in Swanston village in the Pentlands they are everywhere: it is a chocolate-box picture come to life. Deep eaves overhang the tiny windows of the delightfully haphazard whitewashed cottages which form a small cluster near a chattering burn. Surrounding trees protect the minute hamlet from the bitter winds that can sweep across the hills.

At the heart of the seventeenth-century community is the old School House, more ostentatious than the other buildings with two storeys and a roof of slates replacing the thatch. Standing a little apart is Swanston Cottage, the summer retreat of Robert Louis Stevenson,

Robert Louis Stevenson's home in Swanston Village

which he used as the setting for much of his novel *St Ives*. Hardly a cottage by the standards of the rest of the village, Stevenson himself described it as a 'rambling infinitesimal cathedral'. Today its quiet is only disturbed by the clonk of golf balls from the surrounding courses.

The group of nineteenth-century slate-roofed stone dwellings round three sides of a small green a few paces downhill are disappointing compared with the other cottages; their Victorian origin is firmly defined by the 'V.R.' letterbox in an end wall.

From Swanston, footpaths lead east towards the Biggar Road, or penetrate deeper into the Pentlands to give access to the peaks of Caerketton and Allermuir; visitors are asked to keep out of the way of flying golf balls and grazing sheep.

Until recently, Swanston was separated from Edinburgh by peaceful farmland; now it is even more isolated since the city bypass was built, carving a swathe through the fields. Its only road access is the fly-over built to extend Swanston Road, on the south side of Oxgangs Road. In Oxgangs Road itself on an eye-catching corner is the Hunter's Tryst, a late eighteenth-century inn. During the early 1800s, it was a favourite meeting place for Edinburgh's exclusive Six Foot Club, an élite athletic and social organisation which numbered Sir Walter Scott and poet James Hogg among its members. The inn has now been extensively restored and renovated, and once again serves the purpose for which it was built.

MALLENY HOUSE GARDEN

Gardens do not have to be big to be beautiful. This is amply demonstrated at Malleny House near Balerno, where more than 4000 visitors come each summer to enjoy the two-acre garden with its shrubs, roses and herbaceous borders, and wander through the nine acres of woodland.

Although not open to the public except for special events, the house more than completes the atmosphere of old world charm that pervades the estate, and is well worth examining even from the outside. Typical of a mansion belonging to a well-to-do man in the first half of the seventeenth century, it was built for Sir James Murray of Kilbaberton. Oblong and three storeys high, it is surmounted by steeply-pitched roofs with crow-stepped gables.

Because of later additions and extensions, some of the original work has unfortunately become overlaid, but the east front which faces the gardens is practically unchanged. The present entrance lies in the modern part of the house, but a smaller, older doorway surrounded by an heraldic panel opens on to the gravelled drive.

Parts of the house were believed to have been built in the 1630s, and as King James VI is rumoured to have used Malleny as a hunting lodge, it is likely that remains of an earlier building are incorporated into the present fabric.

Standing sentinal in the middle of the hedged garden are four great yew trees more than 300 years old, probably planted at the time the house was built. The garden was presented to the National Trust for Scotland in 1968 by the late Mrs R.R. Gore-Browne Henderson in memory of her husband, Cdr Gore-Brown Henderson, RN. The covered lych-gate leading into the garden incorporates the family crest, a spread eagle.

ROYAL BOTANIC GARDEN

NO DOGS ALLOWED except guide dogs for the blind

Car parking: West Gate in Arboretum Road

Public Transport: City buses Nos. 8, 9, 19, 23, 27

Open daily except New Year's Day
Weekdays 9.00 until sunset;
Sundays 11.00 until sunset
Planthouses: weekdays 10.00–5.00; Sundays 11.00–5.00

Price Guide: Free

Handicapped: Suitable

Publications: available at Inverleith House

Where to eat: Tea-room adjacent to Inverleith House, April–September

No picnics allowed in the garden

The Royal Botanic Garden must take first priority as the most beautiful and relaxing place in the city, whatever time of year you choose to make the few minutes trip. Simply to walk through its gates is akin to stepping into a world where time stands still. Traffic noises abate, and the senses of sight and smell take over as one meanders – nobody ever hurries here – along the many paths which cross and re-cross the 70 acres of this, the second oldest botanic garden in Britain.

It owes its beginnings to two seventeenth-century doctors, Dr Robert Sibbald, the first Professor of Medicine at Edinburgh University, and his colleague Dr Andrew Balfour. Aware of the healing properties of many herbs and plants, they procured a plot of land little more than 12 yards square near Holyrood Palace with the idea of establishing a physic garden. Such gardens had previously fallen within the province of monastic orders, who for centuries had relied on the miraculous properties of plant life to treat all manner of ills.

The physic garden was so successful that within only six years from its founding in 1670 it was apparent that more land was needed. With the assistance of botanist James Sutherland, who later became Professor of Botany at the University and King's Botanist in charge of the Royal Gardens at Holyrood, the doctors acquired ground attached to Trinity Hospital, where Waverley Station now stands.

There would appear to have been no further development of the garden until John Hope was appointed Regius Keeper in 1761, when he amalgamated the town and royal gardens. Later,

the entire plant collection was moved to a site of about five acres in Leith Walk, now Haddington Place, and was to be uprooted yet again between 1820 and 1823, when the much-travelled plant life was moved to its current resting-place at Inverleith. The Experimental Garden of the Royal Caledonian Horticultural Society was also transferred there in 1864, and a further 30 acres of land surrounding Inverleith House were incorporated into the Botanic Garden.

Around 1890, Isaac Bayley Balfour was Regius Keeper, and it was he who initiated plans for reorganisation and modernisation, and generally laid the basis of the gardens we see today. Major undertakings were the building of a large rock garden, and the erection of new glasshouses, some of which were still in use in 1966.

Eighteenth-century botanical research and teaching facilities were up-dated, and Edinburgh found itself a prominent centre for research into plant life, its identification and classification, the true purpose behind any botanic garden. This became increasingly important as more and more botanical explorers ventured further afield throughout the world, bringing back thousands of specimens for scientific examination.

But science is usually far from the minds of those who come to enjoy the Royal Botanic Garden, which has been cleverly and carefully developed over the years into nine distinct but interrelated components, plus a number of imposing glass houses.

Entering from the East Gate in Inverleith Row, visitors find themselves among the 30 or so varieties of heather which, between them, produce a colourful display which lasts throughout the year.

The rock garden is probably one of the favourite features with waterfalls, streams and stepping stones, narrow twisting paths and odd little corners. It was rebuilt between 1908 and 1914 using stone from Perthshire and Dumfries. The water for the stream and pools is pumped up from the pond lying lower down. The pond area itself was originally a bog, and now provides a cool setting for hardy marsh and aquatic plants, with waterlilies, bullrushes, and other moisture-loving flowers; the natural setting is enhanced by such trees as a weeping ash.

Again less formal than some parts of the garden is the woodland area, with groups of shrubs and trees separated by grassy paths which lead on into the peat garden which comprises irregular ledges supported by peat to retain moisture.

The main part of the garden is occupied by the arboretum, and this relatively open grassy area is a pleasant and shady spot to sit and watch the world go by. Worthy of note is the 25-foot high beech hedge which separates the copse and its many species of magnolia from the

Palm house at Botanic Gardens

demonstration garden with its herbaceous borders.

The exhibition plant houses which were opened in 1967 are fascinating. Six huge inter-connecting houses provide ideal opportunities for closer study of ferns, orchids, cacti, temperate and tropical aquatic plants. Fish live in the pools, and if you can find your way down a little side stairway, there is a basement with a large window which allows you to watch the fish as they swim in their natural element, as well as tanks containing other smaller species.

There are two palm houses. The smaller of the two was opened in 1834, having cost £1,500, and the centrepiece here is undoubtedly the Bermudan thatch palm nearly 200 years old which was successfully replanted when the Botanic Garden was moved in 1822. The larger adjoining palm house was opened in 1858. On the outside of this house are two memorial plaques. One is erected to Isaac Bayley Balfour by his colleagues; the other to John Williamson, for 20 years the Principal Gardener (at Haddington Place) and erected by John Hope in 1781 in appreciation of his 'skill in his profession'. An exhibition hall anonymously donated in 1970 has displays showing different aspects of biology and plant life.

Turning right from the cluster of buildings, the way takes the visitor past the azalea lawn with its infinite varieties, and on to the impressive rhododendron walk. Together with others dotted elsewhere in the grounds, they constitute the largest collection of rhododendrons in Britain, and lead the visitor all the way from the west gate to Inverleith House.

The Estate of Inverleith was first mentioned in a charter by Robert the Bruce in the fourteenth century. It was acquired in 1665 by Sir James Rocheid, then Town Clerk of Edinburgh, and it was one of his descendants who built Inverleith House in 1774 at a cost of £4,100!

In 1822, part of the estate was acquired by the Crown for the Royal Botanic Garden, who were moving from Leith Walk. The Crown later purchased the house itself and added it to the garden, where it became the residence of the Regius Keeper. From 1960, it housed the Scottish National Gallery of Modern Art, but in 1985 was handed back to the garden as an exhibition centre.

Four storeys high, its exterior remains much as it was in the eighteenth century. Basically rather plain and square-looking apart from the bulge of the stair tower on the north face, nevertheless its southern aspect commanded extensive views right over the city before this was somewhat obscured by the surrounding trees.

THE WATER OF LEITH

One of the nice things about deciding to explore the Water of Leith, the little river that chatters its twisting way right through the heart of Edinburgh, is that it can be joined or left at scores of places, depending on whether one wants a hefty hike or a ten-minute dawdle.

Rising in the heather-covered moorland of the north-west Pentland Hills and running into and out of Harperrig Reservoir before meandering through a handful of villages – now joined together by suburban development – the Water of Leith flows for 23 miles before reaching the Firth of Forth in the docklands of Leith itself. In its upper reaches in particular, it provides plenty of clues about the era when it was an important river, supplying power and water to dozens of industrial enterprises and the people who lived and worked along its banks.

Now, thanks to the efforts of the district council, helped by volunteer organisations and conservationists, what had deteriorated into a handy rubbish dump is gradually being given a face-lift, and the bank path is being developed into a walkway. Eventually it will be possible to follow the entire length of the Water of Leith from source to mouth.

Commercially speaking, the river began its usefulness where it joins the Bavelaw Burn at Balerno, the village which was also the terminus for the Balerno Branch railway line in the heyday of industrial traffic. The railway is long gone, but its route, closely following the bends of the river, is partially incorporated into the walkway.

At Balerno can be seen traces of the first of the 70-odd mills which mushroomed along the river valley during the 1700s and 1800s, serving a remarkably wide range of trades, and often changing function, presumably to generate a more profitable product. There were grain mills and sawmills, glue works, tanneries and snuff mills, but most of all, paper mills. These were once vital to Edinburgh's economy, being able to provide an on-the-doorstep service to cope with the demands of the capital's expanding bookbinding and publishing trades.

One wonders which of the mills had the distinction of supplying the paper used in that first-ever edition of the *Encyclopaedia Britannica*, printed in 1814 after a brainwave on the part of an Edinburgh engraver, one Andrew Bell.

Baxters (Bakers') Coat of Arms at Dean village

As the footpath continues along the wooded gorge through the villages of Currie, Juniper Green and Colinton, one passes near the mansion houses whose owners wanted to keep an eye on their mills, or simply to have a country retreat.

Woodhall House, dating from the sixteenth century, came into the possession of Adam Cunynghame in 1629, when he bought the lands of Woodhall and Bonaly, including the tower, manor place, and two mills. A few years later, Charles I appointed him to the Supreme Commission for punishing receivers of Jesuits and hearers of masses. The estate was bought by Sir John Foulis of Ravelston in 1701, and it remained in the family until 1932 when, by a strange quirk of fate, the house was bought by an English Jesuit Order.

Spylaw House, overlooking the picturesque Colinton Dell, was probably built about 1650 and in 1759 became the home of James Gillespie. Then, there was a snuffmill behind and beneath the house, traces of which still exist. Gillespie

Dean Bridge over Water of Leith

Colinton village

really came into its own in the sixteenth century when, with the Water of Leith supplying the power, the city's millers and bakers – or baxters as they were then called – adopted the village as their own. They built up a thriving industry, with eleven mills supplying flour to the whole town.

A tolbooth stood in Bell's Brae next to the Baxters' House of Call, formerly an inn and now a private house, its upper storeys peeping tantalisingly over the present Dean Bridge. The mills and granaries at Dean Village were operated jointly by the city and the Incorporation of Baxters, using the tolbooth as their headquarters.

The narrow bridge spanning the ford crossing was built in 1643 according to the date stone, which also portrays crossed peels, the bread-shovels of the bakers' trade. However, this major highway of its day was in turn superseded by Telford's Dean Bridge in 1832, at that time one of the highest in the world at over 100 feet. This took the old coach route away from Dean Village leaving it isolated, but not forgotten.

made a fortune from the mill, money which was later used to endow Edinburgh's Gillespie Hospital and James Gillespie's School.

The remains of Redhall Castle date from the thirteenth century, one of the many buildings which fell prey to Cromwell in 1650. Redhall House nearby was rebuilt in 1756 by George Inglis with stones from the shattered castle, and is now a children's home.

This section of the walkway swings away from the Water of Leith at Slateford to link up with the towpath of the Union Canal. Completed in 1822, its barges delivered rags and coal for the mills, and loaded stone from the local quarries.

Many of the old mills and granaries have been restored and renovated for office or residential use, while the cobbled streets and old houses are complemented by the blending-in of sympathetically designed homes of the 1980s which add to, rather than detract from, the character of this charming old village. A recently-built hotel stands on the site of the former Bell's Mill, which took its name from a sixteenth-century miller who was granted a charter by the monks of Holyrood to grind their meal. A later mill on the site was still in use until destroyed by fire in the 1960s; the largely undamaged granary and old mill lade have been restored and incorporated into the hotel.

Opposite the hotel at Belford Bridge, a flight of steps goes down to the river bank on the opposite side to the village, and a section of the Water of Leith walkway leads to Dean Path which follows the old coachway back across the ancient bridge. From here a pathway continues to Stockbridge, passing the open Doric rotunda of St Bernard's Well, a mineral spring having curative powers which was discovered about 1780. The temple-like structure, housing the old pump workings, was built by the painter and architect Alexander Nasmyth, and enhanced in subsequent years by the addition of a statue representing the goddess Hygeia.

Tucked deep within a wide loop of the Water of Leith in the middle of Edinburgh, Dean Village dates back to the time of King David who, on founding Holyrood Abbey, granted freedom of trade to the mills at Dean, as well as other privileges elsewhere in the city. Dean Village

The walkway can be joined for its present final stretch at Warriston Crescent, a Georgian Street built around 1820. Taking a more direct route than following the river round all its bends in this heavily built-up part of the town, the path follows the disused railway line past the cemetery and the industrial area of Bonnington, finishing in Coalie Park, near Coburg Street in Leith.

THE SCOTTISH CRAFT CENTRE

Open:
Monday–Saturday:
10.00 am–5.30 pm

Price Guide:
Free

Car parking:
Limited in nearby side
streets

Where to eat:
Royal Mile

Acheson House – the
Scottish Craft Centre

The Scottish Craft Centre, with its constantly changing displays, offers the visitor an insight into work drawn from all parts of the country. The organisation was set up by craftsmen nearly 40 years ago to preserve and develop the heritage of Scotland's workmanship and design, and is based at the seventeenth-century Acheson House adjacent to Huntly House Museum in the Royal Mile. It now represents more than 300 men and women who contribute to displays covering the full spectrum of crafts. Ceramics, pottery, silver and glassware jostle with the products of knitters and weavers to form a comprehensive selection of artefacts ranging from the traditional to the avant-garde. It is well worth a visit.

CANDLEMAKING

Candlemaker Row is a steep curving street, just off the south-east end of the Grassmarket, where once the city's many candlemakers worked at one of the most flourishing of Edinburgh's crafts. Now, when the touch of a switch will flood our homes with light, only one shop remains in the Row to carry on the tradition of selling candles made on the premises.

Thousands of years have passed since the first crude candles were made, but while materials have improved, basic techniques have altered little over the centuries. The more sophisticated shapes, designs and colours produced today are the modern candlemaker's response to a market whose demands are for the decorative rather than the practical.

The oldest method of candlemaking is by dipping. First, the appropriate thickness of wick is selected to suit the breadth of the finished article. A fat chunky candle needs a thicker wick than a thin taper: if the wick is too small, the candle will be flooded with excess wax; too large, and the wick will burn itself into a smoky flame.

The paraffin wax comes in either block or powder form, and varies slightly from white to cream in colour. The type most generally used melts at about 56–58°C, but during candlemaking it is heated to a temperature of 82°C to make it fully liquid.

The wicks are dipped in the liquid wax, lifted out for 30 seconds to allow the wax to solidify, then dipped again. The process is repeated, building up the layers until the candle is thick enough to be hung up to cool and harden. If the container of molten wax is large enough, a number of candles can be made at the same time, by tying one end of each wick to a thin rod and dipping them simultaneously.

If the candles are to be coloured, a two-inch layer of coloured molten wax is floated on hot water (82°C) and the dipping process is continued until the candle has picked up the required depth of colour. This is a more economical method than adding dye to a whole container of wax, and by alternately dipping into different colours, a range of different layers can be built up.

The candlemaker can produce an infinite variety of unique shapes by twisting and working the still-soft wax between the hands, or using a sharp knife to cut away designs or peel back layers in leaf form, revealing colours underneath.

This craft is one which allows greatest possible leeway in experimentation, secure in the knowledge that any rejects can be melted down and used again!

COOPERAGE

A South Queensferry man, Ian Andrews, is bringing an ancient craft back to life with a modern-day approach. Working from his cooperage in the old coach house adjacent to the Hawes Inn, he produces barrels and casks ranging from the functional to the decorative, from home-brew requirements to miniature replicas to sit on the sideboard.

After 25 years as a cooper with a local distillery, Ian was faced with redundancy in March 1985. Now he regards that as a blessing in disguise, for he was able to do what he had always wanted – start his own business, using his skills to revive interest in a shrinking trade and expand into the crafts market.

There is always a faint whiff of whisky in the cooperage, for all the wood used by Ian is the well-matured oak of disused barrels which he buys from another local distillery. Some of the casks having been in service for up to 50 or 60 years, they are thoroughly impregnated!

After the barrels are stripped of their hoops, the staves are cut to size and the wood dressed in preparation for its new function. The miniature barrels, tankards, tubs and jewel boxes need to have the staves mitred to the last millimetre to ensure a tight fit, then the wood is steamed and left in clamps overnight to be pressed into its new shape.

To give added strength to the seams some items, including stools, are glued before being sanded down to give a smooth finish. Brass is used for the all-important hoops, which are cut with a slight overlap to allow for the traditional rivet join. The diameter of the hoop must measure exactly that of the narrowest point where the piece is to be banded. When the soft brass is hammered on to the hard oak the pressure exerted is sufficient to make the hoop splay out to fit snugly over the curve of the barrel.

Yacht varnish gives the pieces their gleaming finish, and the brass hoops are buffed to give a satin finish. Additional woodworking, such as cradles for the little casks, taps, or tankard handles is done on a lathe. Admitting to being a magpie, Ian never throws any scrap of usable wood away, and what may be regarded as firewood by most people is treasure to him!

Similar techniques are used to make garden furniture, garden tubs, or large functional barrels, except that steel (later painted black) is used for the hoops, and the seams remain watertight because continual exposure to moisture makes the wood expand against the pressure of the hoops.

After only a few months, Ian discovered that the cooper's skill, far from dying, is much in demand from the visitors who drop in to watch him at work, and his unique handmade pieces are finding their way to all parts of the country.

Cooper Ian Andrews at work

EDINBURGH CRYSTAL

How to get there:
Car: Situated in Eastfield Industrial Estate at Penicuik, off A701 Edinburgh–Peebles road
Bus: To Penicuik from St Andrew Square. During summer, special excursions Monday and Friday, leaving St Andrew Square 1.45

Car parking: Free

Factory Tours:
Monday–Friday, 9.15–3.30; except during statutory holidays and first two weeks in July (children under 10 not admitted on factory tours) Special arrangements for parties and out-of-hours visits. Tel: Penicuik (0968) 75128

Visitor Shop and Cafeteria: open Monday–Saturday, 9.00–5.00

Audio-visual presentations available

Play area for children

One piece of glassware looks very much like another – except at the world-famous Edinburgh Crystal factory. There, you will not find any two items which are identical in every tiny detail, for the very good reason that each one is individually hand-made from start to finish.

Glass has been made in this area for more than 300 years, originally in the port of Leith, when the emphasis was on bottles and everyday drinking glasses. A crystal industry developed during the 1800s at Leith and Portobello, but declined soon after in favour of a return to bottle manufacturing to meet the huge demands of brewers, distillers and wine importers.

The centre for hand-made crystal had by now moved to Edinburgh with the establishment of the Edinburgh and Leith Flint Glassworks. In 1955 it was to be re-named the Edinburgh Crystal Company.

A tour of the Edinburgh Crystal factory is a step into the past, an opportunity to watch the elaborate process of glassmaking by hand, which has changed little since Roman times. Even the techniques and tools used today are inherited almost directly from the skilled glassmakers of two thousand years ago, not through any whim towards the archaic, but because no machine could replace the eyes and hands of the experienced craftsman.

In the glasshouse teams of men, each with his own appointed task, work around the banks of glowing furnaces. Each furnace holds a special fire-clay pot containing the mixture of sand, potash, lead oxide and re-cycled glass that will be fused into molten glass at a temperature of 1400°C. This takes 12 hours, after which it is cooled to 1100°C before being worked.

A ball of molten glass is drawn on to the end of a long hollow tube, which is swung, tilted and twisted as the craftsman blows up the ball of glass to the required size. To ensure uniformity of shape, it is then clamped into an iron mould for a few seconds.

Deftly detached from the original blowing tube and transferred to another holding iron, the vessel has the surplus glass on its neck sheared off while it is still soft. Then comes the tricky job of opening out its mouth, fusing on more molten glass to make a handle, or adding a stem and foot, depending on what is being made.

All this is accomplished very quickly by the team so that the glass, still glowing, can be hurried into a cooling chamber. Gradual heat reduction is essential in order to prevent the glass from becoming brittle or shattering. All being well, the article goes forward to the cutting room, where the bulk of the factory's output is decorated with one of the traditional designs which have made Edinburgh's crystal so famous. Previously painted guide-lines aid the cutter as he converts the design into three dimensions by holding the glass against a variety of carborundum or diamond-impregnated cutting wheels.

Another process, generally reserved for limited editions or special commissions, is engraving, a highly-skilled technique of decoration using a fine copper wheel to achieve a sculpted effect. A more modern addition to the decorative range is that of sand etching, used for finely detailed designs such as foliage or feathers.

Every piece of the exquisite glassware is minutely inspected before receiving its final seal of approval – the company stamp etched for ever on its base. Then, and only then, will the piece you see being made be allowed to leave the factory.

GORGIE FARM

Car parking: Limited on site, or nearby side streets

Open throughout year: Monday–Friday 9.40–4.30; Saturday 1.00–4.00; Sunday 11.0–4.00

Price Guide: Free. Small per capita charge for school parties by appointment.

Handicapped: 80 per cent access

preparation, providing the farm buildings, ramps, paths, and a cobbled roadway. Lothian Regional Council and the Scottish Office also agreed to help with some of the on-going expenses, and the farm was opened to the public the following year.

Very much a project aimed at bringing together all sections of the population, Gorgie City Farm is run by a committee of local people liaising with the five full-time members of staff, and could well be described as an open-air community centre.

Looking after the livestock is the most popular task for the squads of local children who descend on the farm daily, as well as the many others who come either individually or with school parties. There is always plenty to do. There are goats to be milked, the Shetland and Jacob sheep to be admired, and the pigs to be mucked-out! Favourite among the pigs is the sow which appeared some years ago in the BBC's documentary series about life in an Iron Age settlement. Rabbits, guinea-pigs, chickens, turkeys – they are all there to be stroked and admired, while the long-suffering hens no sooner lay their eggs than they are deprived of them so that they are ready for sale to the steady stream of local residents who help support the farm by buying the produce from the vegetable garden.

It is unusual, to say the least, to find a farm – albeit a rather small one – alongside the main shopping street of one of the city's older suburbs. An outsize mosaic mural on the gable end of an adjoining building spells it out in words and pictures: GORGIE FARM. The amount of activity which generally goes on there would do justice to a considerably larger establishment.

There has always been a particularly strong community spirit in the Gorgie and Dalry area of Edinburgh, and in the spring of 1977 local people thought it might be possible to develop a derelict site to provide residents, particularly children, with the opportunity of enjoying and caring for animals in a part of town singularly devoid of parks or fields.

It took five years to persuade officialdom that this was a good idea, but in 1981 the Scottish Development Agency came to the rescue by agreeing to do a considerable amount of site

Not everyone calls in just to buy potatoes or admire the piglets. The more enthusiastic are liable to find themselves mending fences, painting huts, or humping stones for the garden area fronting the street, which was laid out in the summer of 1985. Another attraction, especially for the older generation, is the herb garden.

The most recent addition to the farm was the acquisition of an adjoining disused building. This now provides refreshment facilities for visitors, and a farm shop. A workshop caters for hobbies, in particular homecrafts, joinery, and country crafts; and there is also a project room available for use by school parties.

GREYFRIARS BOBBY

One of the best-known of all doggy stories, and one which has been told, re-told, and romanticised to an extraordinary degree is that of Greyfriars Bobby.

A perky little Skye terrier belonging to John Gray, a Victorian police constable living off the Cowgate, Bobby was trained by his master to be a working police dog. One of his duties was to guard overnight the livestock being brought to the weekly Wednesday mart in the Grassmarket, deterring any potential rustlers with a sharp bite on the legs.

In the late autumn of 1857, John Gray contracted TB and, despite the efforts of the police surgeon, he died early the following year of galloping consumption at the age of only 45, and was buried in Greyfriars Churchyard. After the funeral, Bobby was taken to his old home but, howling his protest, he scampered back to the churchyard. For the next 14 years, the faithful Bobby kept vigil day and night by his master's grave, only leaving when he wanted food, despite the efforts of the churchyard gardener James Brown to enforce the No Dogs rule. Eventually James Brown conceded victory to Bobby, and provided a sack for him to sleep on underneath a table tomb close by John Gray.

When the constable had been alive, it was his custom on market days to have his dinner at Traill's Dining Rooms, and it was here that Bobby went to beg for scraps. Traill was always ready to make sure the dog had plenty, admiring his love for his late master, but after a few years Traill was taken to court for harbouring an unlicenced dog. As the pathetic little story unfolded, the Provost ordered that charges be dropped against the man and went so far as to buy a collar for Bobby with an engraved brass nameplate, thus ensuring future licence immunity. The little terrier was allowed to continue his vigil until he died in 1872, and was buried alongside John Gray. His collar and feeding bowl are now on display in the Huntly House Museum.

Bobby's faithfulness has always had special appeal far and wide; indeed, some years ago a travesty of a film appeared with Lassie in the starring role, and pseudo-Scots-American accents in the taverns of the Cowgate.

Edinburgh folk much prefer to remember the little fellow as he appears today, a charmingly sculpted memorial at the junction of Chambers Street and George IV Bridge, near the pub which bears his name. He is so much part of Edinburgh's scene that after a car knocked him off his plinth on November 1st, 1985, the Highways Department where he was 'hospitalised' reported a number of callers anxious about his state of health. Fortunately he only suffered a grazed back, and a smudge of yellow-line paint on his head, both of which were satisfactorily cured.

HARPSICHORD COLLECTION

The elegant concert hall at St Cecilia's Hall, Cowgate

Car parking: Restricted

Open to public:
Wednesdays and Saturdays 2.00–5.00 During Edinburgh Festival: 10.30–12.30 daily

Price guide: A

Further information on year-round concerts available from Faculty of Music, Edinburgh University. Tel: 031-667 1011

Among the dark and dingy buildings of the Cowgate, one would hardly expect to find a gallery containing a selection of early keyboard instruments that must surely be unique, providing an historic survey of the development of such instruments in the centuries before the modern piano came into being.

The Raymond Russell Collection of Harpsichords was presented to the Music Faculty of Edinburgh University by his mother in 1964, in memory of her son who had always wished to see his collection as a live museum in which the instruments would be restored and played as well as displayed. Now housed in St Cecilia's Hall, Cowgate, the collection has been added to by the University and numbers about 40 pieces, ranging from a 1585 virginal to a pianoforte of the 1800s and includes clavichords, spinets, and harpsichords. Many of them are lavishly gilded and lacquered, the up-raised lids themselves often showing landscapes and pastoral scenes.

Work is continually being done by the Music Faculty on aspects of construction and stringing of these irreplaceable old instruments. The aim is to restore them as nearly as possible to their original state. A number of the instruments are in use, either for demonstration to visitors to the gallery or, more importantly, taking their place in the concerts which are held throughout the year in the hall.

It is singularly appropriate that the collection should have come to rest at St Cecilia's, as it is the oldest purpose-built concert hall in Scotland. Erected for the Edinburgh Musical Society in 1762, it provided a permanent home for the Society's members who until then had met in the back room of a local tavern, and also a nearby chapel.

When the two-storey structure was built by architect Robert Mylne, South Bridge which now runs over the Cowgate did not exist. The bridge's construction in 1785–87 meant the disappearance of all the adjacent buildings with the exception of St Cecilia's Hall.

Interest in St Cecilia's inevitably declined, the last concert being given in 1798 after 25 years as the centre of Edinburgh's musical life. The Society sold it a few years later to the Baptists who used it as a meeting place until the Grand Lodge of Scotland bought it as a Freemasons' hall in 1809. The premises were extended and the elegant oval concert hall with its domed ceiling was made into a rectangular meeting-place, thus completely changing its character.

The next change in ownership came when the Town Council bought it for use as a school. Fifty years later it changed hands yet again to be used as a stationery-making and bookbinding factory owned by one Andrew Cairns. He gave it to his daughter who eventually rehabilitated the building and turned it into a public dance-hall. Intending the premises to be used once again for concerts as well as a dance-hall, Miss Cairns improved the decor in an attempt to restore its eighteenth-century elegance, and in 1959 the first concert for 160 years was held there.

In the same year, the University of Edinburgh had the opportunity to acquire St Cecilia's as an eminently suitable home for the Raymond Russell Collection. Further alterations were carried out to restore the hall to its original oval shape, albeit slightly smaller than the original Mylne design, and extend the buildings still further to provide teaching and practice rooms. Re-opened in 1968, St Cecilia's Hall has once again become the focus of serious musical life in the city, with the emphasis on the composers and the instruments for which the hall was originally intended.

BUTTERFLIES

How to get there:
Car: A7
Galashiels–Carlisle road
6 miles from Princes St;
right-hand side at
Dobbie's Garden and
Nursery Centre, near
Lasswade
Bus: Nos. 80 or 81
Scottish Omnibuses, from
St Andrew Square

Car parking: Free, ample

Open: April–October
daily from 10.00

Price guide: C

Facilities: Gift shop,
bookshop, cafe
School parties welcome:
Telephone 031-663 4932
Play area. Facilities
available for handicapped

Tropical splendour is the description which leaps to mind on a visit to the hot and humid greenhouse which is home for the exotic inmates of Scotland's first butterfly farm. Many people are under the delusion that such establishments are simply collections of lepidoptera, to give butterflies their Sunday name, spread out and pinned in glass cases. Nothing could be further from the truth. Here, one instinctively ducks as fragile wings brush past, for at any one time there are likely to be somewhere around a thousand or more butterflies and moths flying freely among the vegetation and the visitors.

The farm, in its huge purpose-built greenhouse, was introduced to Edinburgh by David Barnes, managing director of a local garden centre, who was so impressed by similar farms in England that he decided to try and bring a small part of the tropics to the chillier climes north of the border. He succeeded, and the venture was opened to the public in April 1985.

Basically a commercial tomato house, the glass structure is completely lined with fine synthetic fibre netting which allows for light and ventilation, but prevents the butterflies dashing themselves against the windows. Splashing waterfalls and ponds combine with high temperatures to produce the humidity necessary for successful cultivation of the many tropical plants on which the insects live, feed, and lay their eggs.

On entering the garden, visitors find themselves in an arbour surrounded by dense foliage, and confronted by a stone feeding table bearing offerings: a squidgy mess of fruit on which many butterflies feed. The winding path crosses an ornamental bridge over the little stream leading to a pond, united in turn by a tiny waterfall to a bubbling mud spring. Its 'bloop bloop' is somewhat startling to the unprepared passer-by, but it rarely fails to fascinate both visitors of all ages and the many species of butterfly which sip appreciatively at the salts in the mud. These salts apparently have the effect of triggering off their fertility cycle, so it's quite a busy place.

Unlike the tropical houses of botanic gardens, the very minimum of pruning and tidying up is done here. Apart from the fact that the caterpillars are very useful for stripping down many of the plants for food, the aim is to encourage a mini-jungle where weeds are as important as the passion flowers as part of the insect diet. In this way, it is possible to simulate the natural habitat of the butterfly during its whole life cycle, even of those which originate in such faraway places as Indo-China, Malaysia, Central and South America, Sri Lanka, Mexico, Indonesia and Japan.

Conscious always of the need for conservation, the farm curator will explain that although there are generally about 50 different species of butterfly ranging free week by week, only the most common varieties are caught and bred. Too many of these beautiful creatures have been lost in recent years through the destruction of natural habitats where caterpillar food-plants were once found, and changes in farming and forestry methods which have proved too drastic for the butterfly to adapt and survive.

Adjoining the hothouse is an exhibition room which explains the natural history of the butterfly with the aid of visual displays.

The exhibition room also houses the 'nasties', safely secured behind plate glass. There is nothing particularly saintly about the praying mantis, for instance. The female being the aggressive one, she is likely to regard a potential husband as an extra meal, and unless he can catch her unawares, she will do just that, and eat him – starting by biting off his head!

The red-legged tarantula is not the sort of spider one would welcome crawling up out of the plug hole in the bath, especially if it is female. They frequently live for about 25 years, whereas the males only survive for about seven years. In captivity, the tarantula is fed on locusts, crickets or cockroaches, but in the wild they have been known to take small birds.

There are other equally unpleasant exhibits in the Insect Gallery which evoke squeals of horror or fascination from the outsider looking in, but it is a worthwhile reminder that all of nature is not necessarily beautiful.

NEWHAVEN AND GRANTON

The scores of fishing boats sailing nightly from Newhaven have now dwindled to a dozen or so, and the cheerful cry of 'Caller Herrin!' from the brightly-clad fishwives in their traditional costumes has not been heard in the city streets for the past twenty years. The village near the great dockland area of Leith still survives, however, a re-development scheme in recent years having restored the old cottages or replaced them with equally attractive homes huddled in the original cobbled streets. The character has been retained by employing red pantiled roofs and outside stairs to upper flats.

Newhaven traces its development from the construction of a royal naval dockyard at the beginning of the 1500s. Its life as a shipbuilding centre was a short one, but the fisherfolk continued as a close-knit community, the oldest institution in the village being the Free Fishermen's Society formed in 1572 for the relief of the destitute and protection of its members.

In the 1700s, the flourishing white fish harvest was expanded when the men were allowed to start dredging for oysters, mussels and clams, and the village's reputation as a centre for shellfish began. An Edinburgh wine merchant, Thomas Peacock, realising the potential of this new market, opened a hostelry specialising in these delicacies in 1767, a tradition still carried on at premises bearing his name.

Until 1878, the fishermen were hampered in bad weather by the insufficient harbour protection of only one pier, but in that year the pier was extended and the west breakwater built. The covered market, replacing that on the open pier, was opened in 1896 and is still the city's main fishmarket. Also still in use is the 1875 Victoria School, barely changed since it was built. Westwards along the shore a public house stands on the site of the 500-foot long chain pier which for some years served small steamer ferries plying to and from South Queensferry.

For a brief period, Newhaven enjoyed the distinction of being Scotland's most important ferry, import and export centre, but after the advent of the railway in the mid-1800s, the village was overtaken by the growth of Granton to the west, leaving the fisherfolk again reliant on the sea's produce for their livelihood.

Granton Harbour, built by the Duke of Buccleuch on his own land, was opened in 1838. Four years later Queen Victoria landed there for her first official visit to Scotland. An interesting detail noted on a fairly recent city map was the inclusion on the western breakwater of Esparto Wharf, a reminder of an import vital to the papermaking industry.

The extension of the Edinburgh–Trinity railway in 1848 opened up the east coast route as it existed before the Forth Rail Bridge was built. The route proved so popular that within six months more than 480,000 passengers used the line.

Granton to Burntisland was the world's first train ferry, involving a complicated operation whereby the coaches had to be transferred to the paddle steamer by a contraption of ramps and moving platforms to cope with varying tides. From Burntisland, the North British Railway Company took the trains across Fife to Tayport, and by a further train ferry to Dundee. The old railway embankment runs between Lower Granton Road and the shore for part of the stretch between Newhaven and Granton, with access through arches set at intervals in the embankment wall. The pathway is neglected and overgrown, but it does provide views of the estuary and the many piers which poke into the sea along this part of the coast.

Granton's trains and ferries are a thing of the past – what matters now are the 250,000 tonnes of cargo, mainly for the oil industry, which the tidal harbour handles annually. It has none of the attraction of the old Newhaven village, and apart from the businesslike aspect of the harbour, can only offer an industrial estate of discount warehouses and wholesalers, overshadowed by the great green towers of the gasworks errected in 1873.

The redeeming feature of a walk or drive through this unprepossessing area is that the road eventually follows the pleasant wide promenade leading to the complete contrast of the delightful village of Cramond.

THE 'GREAT MICHAEL'

The most ambitious and certainly the biggest project ever undertaken at the fishing village of Newhaven was the result of King James IV's decision to have his great four-masted flagship built there. Leith not having enough depth of water, it was decreed that a new royal dockyard be constructed just along the coast at the New Harbour. James was determined to have a Scottish fleet of his own, and shipbuilding became one of his greatest extravagances. He spent more than £15,000 a year on building a navy – in the early sixteenth century this was a large proportion of the country's meagre budget.

It took six years to build the mammoth wooden flagship of the fleet. Named the *Great Michael*, the ship was launched in 1511, at a cost to the king of £30,000. Much of the money went abroad: she was designed by a Frenchman, Jacques Terrel, Norway supplied wood for the masts and spars, and the cordage came from France. The guns and some of the gunners were Flemish, also the source of much of the minor detail, such as candlesticks and lantern sconces. Even the craftsmen who built her were mainly of French origin.

The *Great Michael*'s five decks had gun-ports pierced for 112 guns, and the open upper decks were provided with netting to shield the crew from falling debris and hopefully give some protection against boarding parties from enemy ships.

Crewed by 1,420 men, the ship must have given its catering officer some headaches. Records tell us that when she sailed, she was provisioned with 3,000 gallons of ale, 200 stones of cheese, 5,300 fish, and 13,000 loaves. Rather spartan rations for a fighting force.

The Great Michael

An English Navy Warship, contemporary with The Great Michael

Unfortunately, this dignified ship had a somewhat undignified career. When war was declared between Scotland and England in 1513, James IV's navy was ordered to support the French, already at war with England. Arriving too late to assist their French allies, most of the ships returned to Scotland; *Great Michael*, however, was bought by the French. From then on, the flagship's name disappears from history, and it is likely that she was left to rot in Brest harbour.

Newhaven did not forget its participation in the shipbuilding industry, however. Still preserved near the post office is a sculpted stone showing five nautical instruments of the sixteenth century, surmounted by a representation of a ship which may or may not be the *Great Michael*. Bearing the date 1588 and the words 'In the Name of God', it is regarded by local legend as a reminder of Newhaven's possible contribution to the defeat of the Armada in that year. The stone's obvious tribute to the village's maritime connections is repeated on the primary school wall, where an exact replica cast in bronze forms the memorial to those who died in the Second World War.

Musselburgh & Portobello

Musselburgh got its name from the great mussel bank that used to exist at the mouth of the river Esk which divides the town in two. Much of the shellfish catch was sent to London in former times, bringing considerable prosperity to the community, but the enthusiasm of the fishermen was their undoing: eventually the beds were over-dragged and the mussels disappeared. The fishermen – who lived in the cottages at Fisherrow around the harbour area – came to rely on the local white fish industry, but when the centre for that market moved elsewhere Musselburgh ceased to be a fishing port and lost much of its former character.

However, new industries began to spring up last century along the banks of the river in the form of Esk Mill, which manufactured fishing nets, the Inveresk Paper Mill, and Brunton's Wireworks, all of which are now known worldwide. The originator of the net mill was one James Paterson. Having watched the fishermen patiently hand-making their nets, he invented and patented a machine which, in conjunction with a Scottish loom, could weave both single and double-knotted nets. These products can now be found wherever there are fishing communities.

Musselburgh has always had great importance as a river crossing place, and a few yards upstream from the bridge which carried the never-ending stream of traffic on the A1 before the bypass opened in 1987 is the old bridge which would have been used by Prince Charles on his way to Prestonpans. The cobbled way between crumbling walls is purely for the pedestrian. Locally referred to as the Roman bridge, it has actually been dated to the early sixteenth century, although its name quite possibly indicates that it replaced an even earlier structure.

It is said that a sailor, returning to Scotland after taking part in the storming of Puerto Bello at Panama in 1739, settled down on the shore near Edinburgh and built himself a house which he called Porto Bello. So the story goes, and indeed Portobello seems to have developed from that date, both residentially and industrially.

A large bed of clay having been discovered, a pottery was established which became so famous that even now, 200 years later, Portobello pottery – mainly kitchen crock-type utensils – is still sought after in junkshops and salerooms.

The fresh sea breezes – bracing even on the warmest of days – and miles of smooth golden sand began to attract the attention of the city dwellers, who were quick to build themselves weekend houses at what was fast becoming a fashionable resort. Bathing machines made their daring appearance on the beaches, and the salt water baths were built. This trend continued in Victorian times. The houses became grander and more imposing, parks and bandstands sprouted, and the original promenade was built. With the later addition of an iron pier and various amusements, Portobello must have been regarded as the jet-set resort of the time.

In time trade fell off and the town lost much of its former glory, but today it is enjoying a new lease of life. A grand new promenade now stretches the length of Portobello's foreshore, dotted here and there with gaily-painted seats in easy reach of the main shops, and now that the long-awaited bypass has been completed this once-fashionable resort is beginning to recapture some of the dignified atmosphere of a former age.

'Roman Bridge'

LEITH

The tall houses, some red-pantiled, others with sharply-pointed crow-stepped front gables, which face each other across a narrow stretch of river, could well have come from some old Dutch painting. In fact, they form the new smiling image of Leith, the 800-year-old seaport which serves Scotland's capital, a port whose environs had been allowed to slide downhill for decades but which is now pulling itself up by the bootlaces and coming alive again.

Credit for this rejuvenation must go to the regional and district councils, who called on the assistance of the Scottish Development Agency in setting up the Leith Project in 1981. The aims of the Project include considerable rebuilding and improvements with an eye to Leith's potential as an economic and tourist centre, and also to act as a reminder to Edinburgh folk that the port is an integral part of their history and heritage, no longer to be dismissed as 'the docks'.

Burns' statue at the Corn Exchange

The most dramatic change for the better is in the heart of the medieval port where the tall houses, fringing the Water of Leith before it flows into the estuary, have arisen from the rubble-strewn shells of derelict warehouses. Some have miniature gardens almost to the water-side path; others are fronted by broad sweeps of cobbles.

Intermingling with this domesticity are many old pubs, wine bars and restaurants which are becoming increasingly popular among Edinburgh residents. The number of pubs which abound is partly a consequence of Leith's centuries of trade with the rest of the world, the two most consistent commodities being wine and whisky. The wine connection dates back to Roman times, when the legionnaires guarding the Antonine Wall and the fort at Cramond were provided with wine brought in to Leith.

Much later, the merchants of Leith traded fish for wine, while the monks of Holyrood and other monastic foundations traded hides and sheep. By the 1600s some 250,000 gallons of wine a year were imported – giving James VI a useful boost to his budget to the tune of £32,000 a year from Leith wine alone. Leith's most popular tipple was claret, and in 1985 a special Bordeaux christened The Leith Claret was selected by a group of local publicans and restaurateurs to once again grace the port's dinner tables; the first time in more than 40 years that wine had been shipped direct to Leith from France.

The extra Continental touch of a multi-lingual board pointing to the nearest bus stop is not, however, intended for internationally-minded locals. It is yet another sign of the Leith revival, for increased facilities provided by the Forth Ports Authority in the western harbour now enable cruise liners of up to 25,000 tons to deposit their sight-seeing passengers on Scottish soil.

On the east side of the shore is the old Signal Tower. Once a windmill, it was converted into a watchtower during the Napoleonic wars, and was later used to signal the state of the tides to approaching ships. The tower stands above the landing stage where George IV came ashore on his 1822 visit, an event commemorated now by a brass plaque.

From the nucleus of the new developments on the shore, it is only a minute's walk into Bernard Street, taking its name from Bernard Lindsay, James VI's valet – but don't be deceived by the statue at one end: it's not Mr Lindsay, but Rabbie Burns! Bernard Street became the financial centre for all trading activities and, gleaming bright and fresh after the removal of years of grime, it is at the hub of the most extensive eighteenth-century commercial district surviving in Scotland. A good indication of Leith's prosperity at that time is to be found in the Ionic columns and elaborately decorated ceiling inside the shallow dome of the former Leith Banking Company premises, now used by property developers.

At the corner of Constitution Street and Baltic Street stands the impressive Corn Exchange. Built around 1860 on an old naval yard, the domed Italian-style structure has a striking exterior frieze depicting the grain industry. Trinity House, which now serves as a museum recording the port's maritime history, is situated between Constitution Street and Great Junction Street and may be visited by arrangement.

Lamb's House is a familiar landmark in Burgess Street. Dating from the sixteenth century, it was the home of Andrew Lamb, a successful merchant and personal friend of Mary Queen of Scots, to whom he often extended hospitality during her many journeyings round the country.

Despite the work which has already been done, the Leith Project still has a long way to go. Those behind the Project are determined that the historic seaport of Leith, having been rescued from dusty dereliction, will never again be anything less than a credit to her people and to her capital.

LEITH DOCKS

Nearly two million tons of general cargo are handled each year by the dockyards of Leith. Trade with other EEC countries and with ports throughout the world accounts for much of this, but in recent years the port has become increasingly geared to coping with the complexities of the offshore oil programme.

The Forth Ports Authority, controlling the estuary's two oil terminals as well as its six ports, boasts one of the UKs most important concentrations of oil-related activity, the throughput of piped fuels from the terminals running into millions of tonnes annually. It has fallen to Leith (where the FPA has its headquarters) to play a major part in the provision of dry-docking, heavy engineering, ship repair and conversion, and other facilities or equipment required by supply vessels and oil-related industries.

Leith has long been familiar with handling cereals, particularly those essential to the distillation of whisky. In turn, the export of Scotch whisky is the main reason for many of the regular cargo trips from Leith to ports throughout the world. As a result of this expertise with grain handling, Leith has developed as the Forth's major dry bulk centre, and is equipped with highly-mechanised facilities for the discharge of bulk grain and fertiliser.

Other general cargoes handled at Leith's four interconnecting docks and three harbour berths include general industrial machinery, cars, fruit and vegetables, timber products, coal, and scrap metal. The latter has developed considerably in recent years, and is now the biggest single export commodity from the Forth ports.

Cruise liners are becoming a more familiar sight, and the port acts as host to visiting vessels from foreign navies. It is also the base for two towage fleets, fishery patrol vessels, and Northern Lighthouse Board tenders.

EAST LOTHIAN

The East Lothian coastline

There comes a time when even the most ardent city lover wearies of pounding the streets with aching feet; jostling against crowds; finding somewhere to park the car without attracting the unwelcome attention of wardens.

Relief is at hand, for right on Edinburgh's doorstep are the wide-open spaces of East Lothian, packed full of interesting places to visit and explore. It is an area often overlooked as people rush north or south by the fastest possible means. Surprisingly, the distance via the coast road (A198) from Prestonpans, just past Musselburgh, to Dunbar is no longer than 40 miles; the return trip on the A1 inland is even less. Apart from self-imposed deviations, that is!

Prestonpans could hardly be described as the most attractive place from which to set off on a drive along the coast, but it will always be in the history books for the famous battle of 1745, when Sir John Cope was defeated by Bonnie Prince Charlie on his historic march south. A roadside cairn commemorates the battle now, and several interesting tombstones dating from the event can be found in the cemetery.

The town's name is derived from the local salt panning industry. Since the twelfth century, this was carried on from a priests' settlement round the harbour by heating great open-air pans with locally-mined coal to evaporate sea water. The salt was produced in such quantities that it was sent all over Scotland, and even constituted an export market, albeit limited by today's standards. Until the last century, Prestonpans was also noted for its rich oyster beds, but they dwindled to nothing. Gone too are the other industries of brewing, pottery, brick- and soap-making, and coal mining.

Nearby Prestongrange is the setting for the Scottish Mining Museum, which gives a picture of the 800-year-old industry that had always been vital to the area's prosperity. Occupying a former colliery site, the museum includes the five-floor engine house and the 1874 Cornish Beam pumping engine which can be seen in steam on occasional open days.

Aberlady was once a thriving anchorage for foreign trading ships serving as the port for Haddington, until the river Peffer silted up. It was once the site of a Carmelite nunnery, and the fifteenth-century church is a good landmark with its tall square tower. In the vaulted vestry is preserved part of an early Celtic cross, while at the gate stands the 'loupin-on stane' (mounting block) to assist the more rheumatic worshippers back into their saddles.

Overlooking the sweep of Aberlady Bay is Luffness Castle, supposed to have been the site of a Norse camp, but the old moat and extensive fortifications point to the present castle being mainly sixteenth-century. Vintage car enthusiasts should take this opportunity to visit the Myreton Motor Museum, a short detour from the main road.

The village of Gullane owns five of the 13 golf courses on the coast between Prestonpans and Dunbar, the most famous being Muirfield. With a stretch of sandy beach backed by an expanse of dunes, the village itself is charming – although becoming increasingly built-up as a commuters' dormitory town for Edinburgh.

The Scottish Mining Museum

Dominated by a thirteenth-century castle, Dirleton, with its pantile-roofed cottages surrounding two triangular village greens, has been described as the prettiest village in Scotland. The ruins bear witness to an eventful history, the castle having been bounced backwards and forwards between the Scots and the English before eventually falling to Cromwell

Myreton Motor Museum

The Scottish Mining Museum

during an attack in 1650. Yew trees surround a seventeenth-century bowling green and doocot (dovecot) said to house more than 1000 nests, while nearby is a magnificent Renaissance mansion of the same period.

This part of the coast, which includes Yellow Craig Park, was a favourite resort for Robert Louis Stevenson, who featured the area in a number of his books.

North Berwick is to Edinburgh folk what Brighton is to Londoners – somewhere to go for the day or somewhere to have a weekend retreat. An ancient fishing port clustered round two bays, and a royal burgh since about 1400, the pleasing blend of Victorian and Edwardian architecture gives it that air of a more leisurely age. All water sports are popular here, as well as the inevitable yachting and golf, and the necessary equipment can be hired by those who aren't content to just sit and watch. A sure attraction for the younger generation is the lifeboat donated by one of the many *Blue Peter* appeals.

This modern resort has its darker side, however. Superstition gives it credit for having been the centre for witchcraft in that part of the world, and blood-curdling tales have been told of the activities of these witches and wizards before they themselves were put to death.

Worth a visit, too, is the nearby Berwick Law, a volcanic cone which is part of the same geological fault which threw up the Bass Rock. Topped by a tower built as a lookout against Napoleonic invaders, there is also an inexplicable archway made from the jawbones of a whale.

From the Law, one can see the dramatic ruins of Tantallon Castle, a fourteenth-century fortress standing alone and dignified, with a sheer drop to the sea on three sides. Besieged for much of 1528 by James V until he probably gave up in despair, the castle – despite its fourteen-foot thick walls – was finally destroyed in 1651 by General Monk.

Pilgrims by their thousands used to travel from all over Europe to the fifteenth-century village of Whitekirk to take water from the Holy Well, discovered in 1294 but now no more. The small but attractive church was fired in 1914 by those relatively modern fighters, the Suffragettes, but has been restored. Beside it is an interesting sixteenth-century double-storey tithe barn originally used by the monks of Holyrood as a grain store.

Just outside Dunbar are the two attractive villages of Belhaven and Tyninghame. The former is enhanced by a brewery, the latter by the ruins of St Baldred's Chapel, presumably used by him before his retreat to the Bass Rock.

Popular as a holiday resort, reputedly one of the sunniest in Britain, Dunbar is still an active seaport though considerably less busy than it was three centuries ago when the herring fishing attracted 20,000 workers. It also has a reputation for having been a great smuggling centre – 8,000lb of tobacco were landed there in 1765. Overlooking such activities, innocent or otherwise, are the scattered ruins of Dunbar Castle – scattered because when Oliver Cromwell, having chased the Scots out of town in 1650, made a donation towards the building of a new harbour wall to be named after himself, most of the stones for that wall were taken from the conveniently knocked-down castle.

Probably the oldest Scottish civil building still in constant use is the seventeenth-century Town House in Dunbar. Another fine building in the town is Lauderdale House, one of Robert Adam's many designs; it is now put to commercial use, but its elegance is unimpaired. Also in the High Street is the gabled seventeenth-century tolbooth, boasting a six-sided stair-tower with two clocks and two sundials, surmounted by a slightly lop-sided steeple roof.

Heading back towards Edinburgh from Dunbar and having rejoined the A1, the sea is left behind and the scenery changes to one of gently folding hills and plains. But the visitor shouldn't leave the area without deviating for the clamber up Traprain Law, the third plug in the volcanic ridge, for a last look round at the impressive views.

Reaching East Linton, there is a delightfully picturesque old water mill, Preston Mill, used commercially until 1957. It is still in working order, complete with mill lade and duck pond. The Phantassie Doocot, also well preserved, stands in the grounds of what was Phantassie mansion where John Rennie, the engineer and designer of London's Waterloo Bridge, was born in 1761. Nearer home, he was responsible for the graceful bridge over the river Esk at Musselburgh.

The Phantassie Doocot

Preston Mill

Hailes Castle still retains many of its thirteenth-century features, including the fearsome prison pits into which you can descend by the ladders provided – if you like that sort of thing!

Before reaching Haddington, pay a quick visit to Athelstaneford, where the Scottish flag of St Andrew always flies. Many and varied are the stories and dates surrounding the origin of this tradition, but legend proclaims the sudden appearance in the sky of a white cross on a blue background, a 'sign' to the local populace that this should be the design of the Scottish saltire (flag of St Andrew). Perhaps it would be as well to credit the vision to some over-zealous ancient patriot.

Nearby East Fortune has a bustling Sunday market, many traders coming each week from as far afield as Tyneside, but the old aerodrome on which it is held is more famous as the starting place for the airship R34s first double Atlantic crossing in 1919.

Gifford, south of Haddington, is noteworthy for its air of peaceful charm, and also the fact that the first President of Princeton University, the Rev. John Witherspoon, was born here in 1723. He was the only man of the cloth to sign the American Declaration of Independence. A mile or so away is Yester House, in whose grounds lie the ruins of a thirteenth-century castle with its underground vaulted chamber intriguingly called Goblin Ha'. No-one knows quite why it was constructed – or sunk – but suffice to say that its builder, Sir Hugo Gifford, known locally as the Wizard, was supposedly possessed of supernatural powers. Goblin Ha' was made much of by Sir Walter Scott in his *Marmion*.

In the centre of the rolling agricultural lands of East Lothian is its county town, Haddington, created a royal burgh by King David I, and birthplace of John Knox. Returned to a more leisurely pace since the bypass was completed, this early eighteenth-century town has a number of interesting buildings, as well as being a pleasant shopping centre, the butcher and baker rubbing shoulders with craft and antique shops. Beside the river is St Mary's Church, and a footbridge takes the visitor over the water to Nungate, called after a Cistercian nunnery which once stood there.

From Haddington, the A6093 takes you to the twin villages of Wester and Easter Pencaitland. Near here, set within parkland, is Winton House, a fine example of Renaissance design. Erected in 1620 on the foundations of an earlier house, it has many features of the fortified house with tower and stair-turrets. There the defensive image ends. With ornamental stonework and chimneys, noble apartments and intricate plaster ceilings, it was built at a time when high living was becoming gracious instead of precarious.

And there we come to the end of our Lothian look-about. It is but a short drive to the industrialised township of Tranent from where the main road takes us back to where we started – Musselburgh.

'Taxi!'

The sandy stretches of East Lothian still suffer an annual invasion, but of a very different sort. One day every June the 200 plus taxi drivers of Edinburgh, their cabs transformed overnight into hitherto undreamed-of extravanganzas with flowers, flags, balloons and streamers, give up a day's work – and pay – to take hundreds of needy, physically- and mentally-handicapped children for a day by the sea.

Starting from the main assembly point at Murrayfield Rugby Stadium with a civic send-off, then parading slowly along Princes Street and through Musselburgh, it is an emotional and heart-warming sight to see the expressions of wonder on the children's faces as the scores of cabs head eastwards towards the coast.

On this special day of the Taxi Outing, no-one minds the traffic jams, the city virtually stripped of its cabbies, or the fact that just for once a bus has to be the order of the day.

The Bass Rock

The prospect of more than 9,000 pairs of gannets whirling overhead, as well as guillemots, shags, kittiwakes, and the odd puffin or two, may strike you as being almost too reminiscent of Aldfred Hitchcock's famous thriller, *The Birds*. This, however, is what you must expect if you intend to have a look at the third largest gannetry in the world, situated on that extraordinary volcanic plug of basalt known as the Bass Rock which sticks up out of the sea two miles or so off North Berwick.

The Rock rises sheer from the sea to 350 feet, the guano-draped cliffs reaching up to a grassy plateau a mile in circumference, a pasture which sheep are believed to have once grazed – although how they survived the hoist to the top is anyone's guess.

Birds and animals have not always had the prerogative of sanctuary on the Bass Rock; man, too, has taken sanctuary there over the centuries. The Celtic hermit St Baldred must surely have been the Rock's first human inhabitant some 1,300 years ago, and his cell can be spotted by the sharp-eyed on a terrace half-way up the south side. Later a chapel was built at almost the same place, and when the Bass was granted to a local family in about 1315, they proceeded to build themselves a castle, the ruins of which show obvious good sense in siting since they are on the same ledge as that chosen by modern man to erect the lighthouse.

No doubt because of its grim inaccessibility, the Bass Rock became a state prison in 1671, when at least 50 Covenanting followers were held in the cells, some for as long as six years. Twenty years later, four Jacobite prisoners took revenge on their captors by the simple expedient of locking out the garrison while they were otherwise occupied at the tiny landing place. Comfortably fed and watered by friendly French ships, the one-time prisoners succeeded in holding the Rock for nearly four years.

THE BORDERS

Sheltered to the north by the Moorfoot and Lammermuir Hills and to the south by the Cheviots, a spider's web of roads weaves its way, twisting and turning, through the vast acreage which makes up the Borders country, crossing and re-crossing the river Tweed and its tributaries to link the towns: Peebles, Galashiels, Selkirk, Hawick, Lauder, Melrose, Jedburgh, Kelso . . .

There is an aura of timelessness about this country. The market towns and villages which for centuries stood in the front line of border strife are all busy, bustling communities, but the people are more placid, more relaxed, less obsessed with haste than their city cousins. The most knocked-about and re-built part of the country will always bear the scars inflicted centuries ago, but those scars have mellowed and now merge together as reminders of our heritage. Great abbeys stand in ruins, sad memorials to King David I who founded them, but the lands which once echoed to the yells of warring factions are now undisturbed except for the calls of birds and the sounds of farm animals.

A pleasant country town barely half-an-hour from Edinburgh, Peebles became a royal burgh under a charter granted by David I in the early 1100s. Three hundred years later, the charter was lost or destroyed during an attack by the English, but James II rectified the matter by granting a replacement charter which survives to this day.

Standing high above the town is the Ruined Cross Kirk, founded in 1261 to commemorate the discovery of an inscribed stone and cross which had reputedly been lost since about AD 300. Peebles seems to have an unfortunate knack for losing its possessions. A mile from the town, perched on a rocky outcrop

River Tweed at Peebles

overlooking a bend in the river, is Neidpath Castle. Although built to withstand the heaviest of attacks, it was lost to Cromwell after a long siege.

Traquair House near Innerleithen has the distinction of being not only the oldest inhabited dwelling in Scotland, but the only building to have housed the same family for nearly 500 years. Through the centuries since 1100, Traquair has sheltered 27 English or Scottish monarchs, ownership of the house bouncing from one royal favourite to another. In the late 1400s, it became the property of the Earl of Buchan, an ancestor of the family who live there today, the Maxwell-Stuarts.

Visitors may wonder why the great Bear Gates guarding the main drive are always locked. After Bonnie Prince Charlie had passed through them on his way south to claim the crown, the fifth earl had the gates closed after him vowing that they should remain locked until a Stuart king again sat on the Scottish throne. By family tradition, that promise has been kept.

Near the source of Yarrow Water, one of the river Tweed's many tributaries, lie two stretches of water, St Mary's Loch and Loch of Lowes, separated by a peninsula on which sits the historic Tibbie Shiel's Inn. St Mary's is the largest loch in the south of Scotland. This beauty spot would appear to have been poets' corner in the Borders, for it was a favourite meeting place for Scott, Robert Louis Stevenson, Thomas Carlyle, and James Hogg – perhaps better known as the Ettrick Shepherd – whose statue gazes out over the rippling waters.

Traquair House

Windsurfing on St Mary's Loch

caters for students from all over the world, working in the realm of fabrics, design, and textile-related art forms.

One cannot envisage the Borders without Abbotsford, the treasure-filled country house which was Sir Walter Scott's home for 20 years. A romantic by nature, with an intense love for the area, Scott achieved his ambition of becoming a Borders laird when he paid 4,000 guineas for the small farm and steading of Cartleyhole in 1812. Since it was situated on the banks of the river Tweed near a place once used by monks to cross the river, he changed the farm's name to the more dignified Abbotsford. Logical, if not original.

A few miles further on, just over the border into Dumfries and Galloway is the impressive waterfall known as Grey Mare's Tail, tumbling from its source high in the hills at Loch Skeen.

Galashiels owes much of its present prosperity to the textile industry, and to Sir Walter Scott's outrageous daring in appearing on the streets of London wearing a pair of trews made from the traditional black and white Borders shepherds' check. London society was shocked, but this new fashion caught on and soon everyone was wanting them, giving the necessary boost to a flagging industry which has never looked back since.

Galashiels' name and tradition of cloth-making goes back for centuries, to the days when herdsmen built summer shelters, or shielings, on the banks of Gala Water so they could watch over their stock at summer pasture. Meanwhile their womenfolk undertook the spinning and weaving which were their other means of livelihood. The craft grew into an industry, the shielings gave way to textile mills, and following Scott's timely demonstration of social bravado the industry became so important that, in 1909, the Scottish College of Textiles was established there. It now

Abbotsford

At first, he contented himself with building extensions to the existing farmhouse, but in 1822 the increasing income from his writing prompted Scott to demolish the original property and start all over again by building the main block of the new Abbotsford on its site. From then on, depending on the state of his finances, the structure was enlarged in random stages. Scott's mania for collecting anything collectable came to the fore as he incorporated into the building a door from Edinburgh's old Tolbooth, carved oak from Holyrood and Dunfermline Palaces, and Roman reliefs from Hadrian's Wall.

Three miles up the Ettrick valley from Selkirk is Bowhill, the seat of the Dukes of Buccleuch. Dating from 1812, it is still furnished with many original silk brocades and hand-painted Chinese wallpapers which provide a delicate backdrop to the many other treasures. Visitors can also see a restored Victorian kitchen, and in the grounds there is an adventure park, a tea room and a gift shop.

Abbotsford, home of Sir Walter Scott

Hawick, nine miles south of Selkirk, was for centuries a convenient staging post for passing armies. On one such occasion, on the approach of the invading English, the inhabitants dragged off their roofs, burnt the thatch in the streets, and fled – leaving the troops without board and shelter. Needless to say, the soldiers took their revenge: they finished off the bonfire by razing the entire town to the ground.

The largest of the Border towns, Hawick (or Haga-wic as it was originally known) made a name for itself in the late 1700s as a centre of wool and linen manufacture, the fore-runner of today's thriving fashion knitwear industry.

Lauder, bounded on three sides by the Lammermuir Hills, is a former coaching stop which was designated a conservation area in 1972. The compact main street and market place make the town appear deceptively small at first glance; in fact narrow lanes running off that main street, and recalling its medieval past, lead to more dwellings which were built as needed in the long back yards of the existing houses. The Tolbooth, built about 1318 and still in almost its original condition, presents an odd sight to the passer-by – barred windows on the ground floor. Not to keep people out, but to keep them in, as this was once the town gaol.

Half-a-mile away is Thirlstane Castle, the home of the Maitland family since 1570. Originally a sixteenth-century keep, the building had a forbidding military aspect until Sir William Bruce, the Architect Royal of Holyroodhouse, was called in to transform it into a mansion house. This he did, employing craftsmen brought over from Holland to model the intricate garlands and crowns which adorn the walls and ceilings of the magnificent state rooms. In one wing is the Border Country Life Museum, which shows the development of life in the Borders from prehistory to the present day.

Eildon Hils

Some six miles north-west of Kelso on the road to Gordon lies the gracious Mellerstain House, its two wings built by William Adam in 1725, and the centre block completed by his son Robert some 50 years later. This block includes the library, widely regarded as Robert Adam's masterpiece of interior design.

The superb collection of paintings and period furniture is complemented by the magnificence of the interior decoration, the ceilings being still preserved in their original colours.

Rugby fans do not need to be reminded that the game originated at Melrose, and caught on so fast that it is now regarded as the national sport of the Borders. Melrose lies at the foot of the triple peaks of the Eildon Hills, one of them capped by a Celtic hillfort, and in this beautiful setting David I chose to found the first Cistercian settlement in Scotland. This abbey received the same treatment from the English as its neighbours, and although the monks kept patiently re-building after each bout of destruction, funds ran out before the abbey could be completed. Nevertheless, much fine work survives, including ornamentation with carved fruit and flowers, and caricature-like human figures of artisans wielding the tools of their trade.

Melrose Abbey

A museum beside the abbey contains relics from its past and from the Roman fort at Trimontium (Triple Hills). In a nearby converted farm building, there is a motor museum with a unique collection of some 25 vintage vehicles, old signs and accessories.

Close by Melrose Abbey are the unique Priorwood Gardens. The only gardens of their type in Britain, they specialise in grasses, herbs, and shrubs especially cultivated for drying. Leaflets are also available on how to produce displays of everlasting dried flowers.

Mention July 18th to travelling people and they will immediately pinpoint the date as that of the great annual horse fair which used to be held on the spacious village green of St Boswell's. There is little horse trading done now, but St Boisil's Day is still kept as a meeting date

Riding the Marches at the Jethart Callants Festival at Jedburgh

for hundreds of travellers from all over Scotland and northern England. The old spelling is derived from the name of an early hamlet built on the site of a church, long since vanished, dedicated to St Boisil, a seventh-century prior of Old Melrose Monastery. Strategically important in the Middle Ages, the town once had 16 peel towers surrounding it for defence – they were not very effective however, for the last of them fell during the 1545 invasion!

Jedburgh, a mere ten miles from the English border, still carries the scars of its violent past. The abbey, founded by David I in 1152, was burnt down on the orders of the Earl of Surrey in 1523, and now stands roofless and shattered with only three tiers of arches and the 86-foot high transept tower still standing. In the summer of 1984, archaeological excavations at the red sandstone ruin uncovered the burial ground of the Augustinian abbots, laid in their stone coffins underneath the chapter house floor, and a further burial ground for lesser brethren in adjoining land.

Jedburgh Castle, popular with Scottish monarchs because of its perch high above the town, was also ultimately destroyed by the English. A prison was built on its site in 1823, and this now houses a museum.

Another museum in the town, largely dedicated to mementoes of Mary Queen of Scots, is Queen Mary's House, the fortified tower where she stayed to recover from an illness contracted after a 50-mile gallop over wet and windy moors to visit her lover Bothwell, lying injured at his home at Hermitage Castle. Mary still being married to Lord Darnley at the time, the escapade caused quite a stir.

Hermitage Castle took its name from the monks who used a nearby chapel as a retreat. The most massively-built of all Borders bulwarks, and well equipped with dungeons, Hermitage has a turgid history of murder, mystery, and intrigue – successive owners apparently getting possession by disposing of the unwanted predecessor.

David I's greatest Borders abbey, run by Benedictine monks and reputedly Scotland's richest monastic establishment, was at Kelso. It depended for its defence on Roxburgh Castle on the other side of the river, but the abbey lost this protection when the castle was utterly destroyed following the siege of 1460. It was during this engagement that King James II was killed when one of his own cannon exploded unfortunately close to where he was standing.

Only seven days after his father's death, the infant James III was crowned King of Scotland in Kelso Abbey, and an uneasy peace prevailed for the next century. After the Battle of Flodden, however, Kelso became a ready target for the monotonously regular invasions which culminated in 1545 with the virtual destruction of the abbey by the Earl of Hertford, who killed the 100-strong garrison and left little more than the gabled north transept standing.

Many years later, the town's trade prospered considerably following the building of a bridge over the river. It was modelled on London Bridge by the designer, John Rennie, who was also responsible for the design of the old Leith Docks and the present bridge over the river Esk at Musselburgh.

One must not forget that the Borders country extends eastwards to a dramatic coastline of sheer cliffs, sandy beaches, smugglers' caves, seemingly inaccessible inlets, and fishing ports.

The most prominent feature along this 20-mile stretch is St Abbs Head, whose towering cliffs spell home to numberless seabirds, and is now a nature reserve administered by the National Trust for Scotland. Nearby lies the picturesque fishing village of St Abbs, clustered on the site of a Christian settlement which was dedicated to St Ebba in around AD 600.

Eyemouth has been a busy fishing port for 800 years, with its traditional smoke-houses and flourishing boatyard. The old harbour and sandy beaches make it a popular seaside resort and a good venue for sea-angling, both for pleasure and competition.

INDEX

VANISHING HABITATS

Designed and produced by
Aladdin Books Ltd
70 Old Compton Street
London W1

First published in
Great Britain in 1987 by
Franklin Watts
12a Golden Square
London W1

ISBN 0 86313 592 7

The front cover photograph shows a devastated rain forest in Brazil. The back cover photograph shows squirrel monkeys in the forest.

The author, Noel Simon, worked for the International Union for Conservation of Nature and Natural Resources in Switzerland. He compiled the Mammalia *volume of the* Red Data Book, *the international catalogue of the world's rare and endangered species. He is also the author of many children's books on Natural History.*

The consultant, Michael Bright, is a Senior Producer at the BBC's Natural History Unit, Bristol, UK. He is also author of several books on Natural History.

Contents

VANISHING HABITATS

Noel Simon

Newcastle-under-Lyme College
Staffordshire

Franklin Watts
London : New York : Toronto : Sydney

Introduction

Habitat is the area in which a particular plant or animal lives, the place where the essential conditions for its life exist. A healthy habitat is a basic necessity: it provides air to breathe, water to drink and food to eat. But air and water are being polluted and habitats degraded. Squandering of the earth's natural resources is creating an increasingly ravaged world. And as animals and plants live in delicate balance with their habitat, the degradation of habitat is a great threat to their survival.

Much of the damage to habitat results from the increasing numbers of people. In the third world 500 million people are malnourished and 800 million destitute. Simply to stay alive and avoid starvation these people are degrading their habitat still further by cutting down forests, by overstocking their grazing lands, and by cultivating unsuitable land. In the industrial world, habitats are being degraded by pollution and commercial exploitation. This book looks at the main types of large-scale habitat to be found in the world, as well as at some small-scale examples, and shows what is happening to them. It also points out that the degradaton of habitat poses a threat to the quality of life and ultimately to mankind's own survival.

◁◁ Each increase in human numbers adds to the growing pressures on habitat and natural resources. The rain forests (far left) are destroyed through timber extraction, burning and grazing.

◁ Squirrel monkeys (left) are widely distributed in the rain forests of South America. They feed on lizards, eggs and insects. Animals like these are under threat from the destruction of the rain forests.

The vanishing forests

By the year 2000, one third of the world's tropical rain forest will have been destroyed. Most of this tropical rain forest lies in Brazil. It has had an extremely high rate of growth and a very varied plant and animal life. Amazonia, for instance, possesses one million species of plants and animals. When the trees are cut down, leaving the ground exposed, the plant nutrients are quickly washed out of the soil. Then the land becomes unproductive. And, as most tropical rain forests grow on sterile soil, this process happens quickly. Replanting of trees seldom takes place. Even when it does, quick-growing pines or eucalyptus are usually planted instead of tropical rain forest trees.

Often the forests – which contain valuable hardwoods such as teak and mahogany – are seen only as an endless source of timber for logging and fuel. The timber industry has expanded greatly in the last 30 years and some forests, particularly in South East Asia, have been so exploited that they have been ruined.

▽ The photograph shows the effects of acid rain. Poisonous gases from factory chimneys and vehicle exhausts are carried by winds and fall to earth in the form of acid rain. Forests, lakes and rivers in more than 20 industrialized countries are affected. Half of Switzerland's forests are already dying.

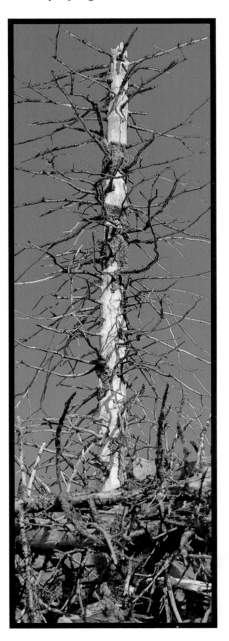

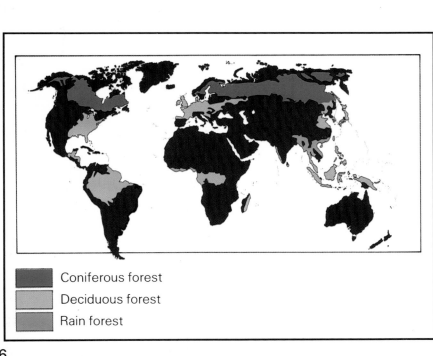

Coniferous forest

Deciduous forest

Rain forest

The largest stretch of coniferous forest in the world – the taiga – encircles the earth in the northern hemisphere. The taiga supplies the bulk of the world's commercial softwood timber. The dominant tree species is larch, but fir, spruce and others are common. Coniferous forest reaches down North America's Pacific coast to California. Some of the world's mightiest trees – Douglas firs, redwoods and sequoias – are found in this area. The greatest threat to coniferous forest comes from acid rain. Huge areas are affected.

Deciduous forest used to cover much of Europe and the whole of the eastern part of North America. Most of it has been destroyed. Typical European tree species are oak, beech, ash and chestnut, together with such animals as the wild boar, red fox, roe deer, badger and squirrel. Typical North American species are the white-tailed deer and the wild turkey. Today what little is left of the original deciduous forest is well preserved, especially in the United States.

△ Tawny owl

▷ A deciduous tree like the one in the diagram forms the habitat for many kinds of animals. But because of differences in feeding habits and behaviour, the various species do not conflict with one another. Some birds, for example, specialize in eating either insects, seeds or fruit. On the forest floor decaying leaves and rotting branches support huge numbers of insects. Badgers dig rodents from their burrows, while deer feed on grass, leaves and shoots. Foxes and weasels, hawks and owls prey upon mice, voles, rats and rabbits. The purple emperor usually spends most of its life in the tops of oak trees. Together, the animals and their habitat form a balanced system – an "ecosystem".

△ Purple emperor butterfly

Rain forests

Destruction of habitat is the single greatest threat to the survival of species. Safeguarding adequate examples of different types of habitat is therefore the most effective measure that can be taken to conserve them. Many rare species — such as the Javan rhinoceros — have survived only because a national park has been created for them. Other animals such as the orang-utan which lives in the tropical forests of Borneo and Sumatra are more at risk from deforestation.

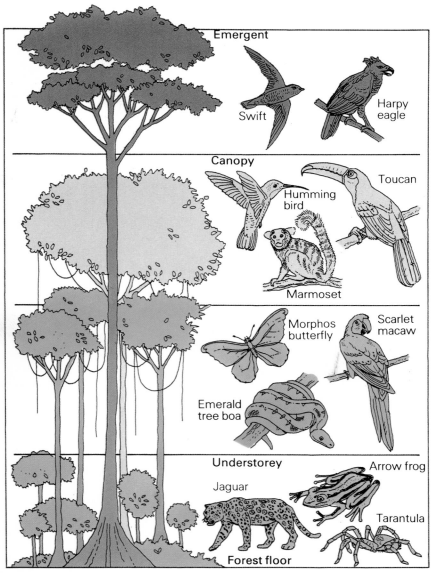

Emergent

Swift

Harpy eagle

Canopy

Humming bird

Toucan

Marmoset

Morphos butterfly

Scarlet macaw

Emerald tree boa

Understorey

Jaguar

Arrow frog

Tarantula

Forest floor

△ Birds of paradise are found only in the forests of New Guinea and nearby islands. They form the most brilliantly coloured group of birds in the world.

◁ The forest canopy is made up of three or more layers. Each consists of the crowns of different types of trees and supports different types of animals. At the lowest level is the understorey. The middle storey, the canopy, reaches to about 36m. Towering above all else is the emergent layer reaching to about 45m. In the Amazonian forests large mammals such as the tapir and the jaguar are confined to the forest floor. The pygmy anteater and the tamandua climb the trees in search of the termites and insects. The canopy supports a wealth of brightly plumaged birds.

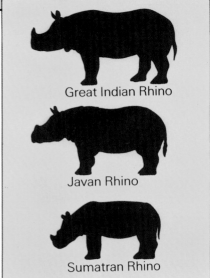

Great Indian Rhino

Javan Rhino

Sumatran Rhino

△ The Javan rhino is extremely rare. Its last remaining stronghold is the Udjong Kulon Reserve on the western tip of Java, where there are about 40 individual animals.

The reproductive rate is low and fears have been expressed that there are not enough births to compensate for losses. The male has one horn — the female none.

△ The Javan and Sumatran rhinos live in dense forest, browsing along the edge of clearings; the Indian rhino prefers swampy jungle, feeding on grass and reeds.

◁ The orang-utan is the only one of the great apes to be found outside Africa. It lives in the tropical forest of Borneo and Sumatra and finds it almost impossible to adapt to any other type of habitat. Loss of habitat, both for logging and to provide more cultivated land for the ever-expanding human population, is splitting the remaining orang-utans into small and often isolated groups, which have greater difficulty in surviving.

The grasslands

The four major grassland regions in the world, the North American prairie, the South American pampas, the Eurasian steppe, and the African savanna have all been intensively exploited and developed. The prairielands of North America were very suitable for cattle ranching and wheat growing. Thousands of acres were ploughed, and thousands more overstocked and over-grazed. Removal of the natural grass cover exposed the soil to the hot sun, causing it to dry out, become sand, and be blown away by the high winds. Today, soil erosion is sometimes controlled by contour ploughing, a technique which prevents the soil being blown or washed away from exposed hillsides.

The vast steppe lands of Central Asia have also been used for cattle ranching and agriculture. The herds of goitred gazelles, wild Bactrian camels, wild asses and wild horses that used to live there have been reduced. They were destroyed partly by unrestricted hunting and partly because the nomads prevented the wild herds from having access to scarce water which they wanted for their own domestic livestock.

The photograph shows bison, or buffalo, one of the animals closely associated with the American prairie. The settlement and development of the prairie a century ago marked the end not only of the bufffalo but also of the Plains Indians whose way of life was closely bound up with the buffalo. Within a few decades the immense buffalo herds, estimated to have once numbered 60 million, had been largely destroyed. When survivors were discovered in Canada, Wood Buffalo Park was established for their protection.

Grasslands

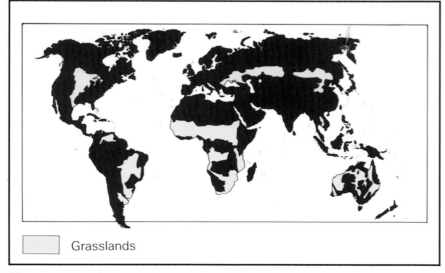

An animal carcass in Africa is the symbol of the expanding deserts. Areas of dry grassland too poor for agriculture are used by nomads and their herds of domestic animals. As numbers steadily increase, overgrazing becomes inevitable. The fragile vegetation is destroyed and the deserts move in on the hooves of cattle, sheep and goats.

"While our prairie grain belt is of great importance to North America no one will ever again see the ecosystem of the grassland that existed there before the white man's settlement."

Charles Caccia
Minister of the Environment,
Canada, 1984

The desert

Until recently, deserts were regarded as wastelands and these served as natural sanctuaries. But the discovery of oil brought dramatic changes. Lands considered useless quickly became among the richest for beneath them lies enormous wealth in the form of oil. However, oil wealth has opened up the deserts to every kind of exploitation. Often, the oil crews relieve their boredom by hunting any wild animals they can find. Poor nomads on horse or camel and rich Arabs in motorized cavalcades have added to the toll. The addax and the slender-horned gazelle, once among the most common animals in the Sahara, have become very rare indeed. In Arabia the ostrich, bustard and cheetah have been exterminated and three species of gazelle almost wiped out. The Arabian oryx was saved from extinction only by capturing the last few survivors.

Deserts are another example of how a habitat can gradually be degraded. And because animals are linked together by food chains, the downfall of one species quickly leads to serious survival problems for another.

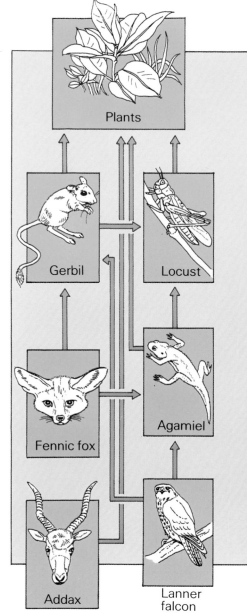

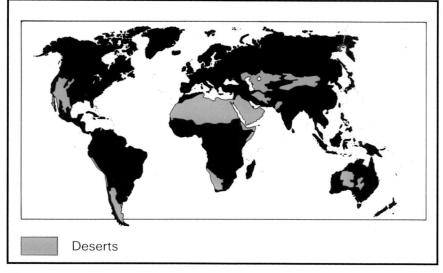

Deserts

△ The base of the desert food chain is formed of numerous insects feeding on plants. Insects are eaten by spiders, scorpions and their small predators, gerbils. Lizards feed on locusts and are themselves the prey of snakes and hawks. Lizards are eaten by the fennic fox which also feeds on gerbils. At the top of the food chain are the big predators, which prey on the large grass-eaters, such as the addax.

"In the name of progress the ecosystems of the third world are daily subjected to torments from the most sophisticated technologies."

Felipe Benavides, Peruvian ex-Diplomat

The Kalahari Desert has only sparse vegetation but the recent expansion of Botswana's cattle industry has greatly increased the numbers of livestock using the area. Long lines of fences have been constructed to control the spread of disease. These fences cut across the traditional migratory routes followed by the herds of wildebeest, zebra, eland, springbok and other species in search of winter grazing and water. Their route blocked, the wild animals die of starvation and thirst on the wire. Losses have been on a huge scale.

△ The addax lives in waterless and uninhabited country deep in the Sahara, so does not compete either with man or his domestic livestock. Properly managed, the addax could be a valuable animal in "converting desert into protein". Instead, it has been nearly exterminated.

The cold wilderness

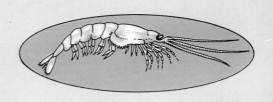

Antarctica, covering more than 12 million sq km, is the only continent to be entirely without a human population. Unpolluted and unexploited, it forms the perfect wildlife sanctuary. The Antarctic Treaty, signed in 1959, outlawed commercial exploitation of Antarctica. Human activities were restricted to genuine scientific work. But valuable oil and other mineral deposits are known to exist there and demands are already being made to allow their exploitation.

△ Fishing for krill — a shrimp-like animal of high protein value — is being massively increased. Krill is a key animal in Antarctica's ecosystem as it is the main food for baleen whales and many seabirds.

▲ Emperor penguins live in the Antarctic and breed in the middle of the Antarctic winter. The single egg is incubated by the male until it hatches. Both parents then take it in turns to look after the chick.

Tundra

Ice caps

... the tundra

The tundra is the largest continuous tract of wilderness and wildlife habitat remaining in the northern hemisphere. But, in 1968, with the discovery of oil near Prudhoe Bay, in Alaska, technology burst upon it. The installation of a 1,300km pipeline, the sinking of wells, road construction, and the movement of heavy equipment created ecological disturbance over a wide area.

In summer the surface of the tundra thaws, leaving the land studded with pools, lakes and marshes. Mosquitoes, midges and blackfly hang above the tundra like a dark mist. Migrant birds come in their millions, attracted by the insect food and the secure refuge. While ducks and geese find rich pastures in the extensive wetlands. Almost constant daylight allows maximum time for feeding – ideal conditions for raising nestlings. More than 100 migrant bird species nest on the tundra, making it the most important bird sanctuary in the world.

Permafrost

Surface meltwater

Permafrost

△ The photograph shows a new tundra highway carefully built to avoid unnecessary damage to the habitat. The tundra consists of two layers, the top layer which is frozen in winter but thaws in summer and the permafrost layer – which is always frozen. Frozen soils are particularly vulnerable to disturbance, and the use of tracked vehicles on the tundra during spring and summer creates gullies, causing soil erosion. This leaves behind permanent scars. The diagram shows how even slight tracks can deepen once the frozen top soil begins to melt.

Arctic life

For thousands of years the Arctic has remained an unspoiled natural sanctuary. But severe climatic conditions are no longer being allowed to stand in the way of development. The northern territories are being opened up for both military and industrial purposes. Exploration, research and development are governed by military requirements such as early warning systems and air bases. The Arctic's mineral wealth is also being exploited.

The polar bear
Male polar bears may be 1.5m at the shoulder and weigh 600kg. Their broad feet have furry soles with the front paws partially webbed. Cubs (usually twins) are born in dens in the ice. Newborn cubs weigh less than 1kg.

△ There are about 10,000 polar bears, mostly in the Canadian Arctic. Much of the polar bear's life is spent at sea among the pack ice: it is an expert swimmer. Its main prey is the ringed seal. In summer when the ice breaks up and seals become scarce, the polar bear moves ashore. Summer is a lean period for the polar bear. Hunger drives it to eat anything it can find – carrion, seaweed, berries, birds' eggs – or even to raid dustbins and rubbish dumps. Apart from subsistence hunting by Eskimos, the species is protected over most of its range. Pollution from off-shore oil drilling and spillage from pipe lines are a danger, but an even more sinister threat comes from the accumulation of lethal quantities of poisonous chemicals in the bears' bodies. These chemicals come from the seals on which they prey mainly during the winter.

△ The caribou – the same animal as the domesticated reindeer of the Lapps and other Arctic peoples – undergoes a seasonal migration into the tundra. In April the herds of barren ground caribou, together with their newborn calves, leave their wintering grounds in northern Canada and trek northwards across the tundra, feeding as they go on the reindeer moss uncovered by the melting snow. After summering in high latitudes and mating during September, the herds – sometimes assembling in groups of several thousand – start the return journey to their winter quarters. The migrating herds of caribou are followed by packs of wolves which prey on stragglers and on the sick members of the herd.

The caribou
Males stand 1.25m at the shoulder (females are smaller) and weigh up to 275kg. Both sexes have antlers. Broad, flat hooves are an adaptation for walking on wetlands and snow. Females produce a single calf after 8 months' gestation.

▷ Both caribou and reindeer have been affected by radioactive fallout, the latter from the accident at the nuclear power plant in Chernobyl, USSR. The reindeer moss (seen in the photograph) on which they feed accumulates radioactive substances which become concentrated in their bodies.

Mountain sanctuaries

People have long been attracted by the beauty of high mountains and tourism has become big business. Getting tourists into the Alps has meant the building of roads and railways, ski-lifts and resorts.

Other man-made developments have affected the habitat. Huge dams have been built to store water from melted snow to be used for irrigation or hydro-electric power. Because intensive development in the lowlands wiped out many of Europe's native predators, the mountains have become the last stronghold for some of Europe's rarest fauna. The golden eagle, the wild cat and the lynx are now almost entirely confined to the more remote mountains.

▷ The alpine ibex lives on cliffs and crags close to the snow line and is astonishingly sure-footed. A century ago the ibex was almost exterminated by hunting. The only survivors were a few in a remote part of the Italian Alps, from which the animal was later reintroduced into Switzerland, France, Austria and Yugoslavia.

"Man is tinkering with his environment; and the absolute requirement of intelligent tinkering is to save all the parts."

Aldo Leopold American Forester, pioneer conservationist and writer

Tourists can sometimes pose a threat to mountain range habitats by damaging soil and vegetation through sheer weight of numbers. Volcanoes, geysers, waterfalls, canyons and glaciers are among the tourist attractions vulnerable to excessive numbers of people. National parks have tried to solve the problems of preserving alpine habitats in different ways. In the Swiss National Park, for example, the number of people entering the park at any time is limited and fishing, shooting and camping are not allowed. The French National Park in the Pyrenees is divided into two zones: an inner area in which no building is permitted, and an outer area with limited tourist facilities.

△ Edelweiss is a plant associated with the Alps. The true flower lies in the centre of what looks like hairy white petals but are in fact leaves. Plants like these are under threat from being trampled or picked by tourists. In many parts of the Alps visitors have to keep to special routes to preserve the soil and the wildflowers.

▷ Before people and livestock could move into the Okavango swamps, the area would have to be cleared of the tsetse fly which carries sleeping sickness. But spraying with insecticides not only destroys the fly. It is lethal to many birds, reptiles, small mammals and fish. It even destroys certain plants by killing their pollinators.

The wetlands

◁ The Okavango Swamp is an 18,000sq km floodplain in Botswana. The human population has increased so much that people west of the delta want to leave their overgrazed lands and move with their cattle into the delta proper. Plans have also been made to construct canals to carry water from Okavango to mining areas. These proposals could spell the end of Okavango as a wildlife sanctuary.

▽ Water birds abound in the Okavango floodplain. Resident birds include herons, spoonbills (seen in the photograph) and fish eagles. The swamps are also the wintering ground for large numbers of migratory ducks and geese.

All over the world wetlands are threatened by drainage and conversion to arable land. This has been encouraged by the mistaken idea that wetlands are wastelands. In fact they are a highly productive type of natural habitat. As well as producing quantities of fish, wildfowl and reeds wetlands serve as natural reservoirs. They accumulate and store water in wet periods and release it during dry periods. Wetlands are also ideal bird sanctuaries because of the abundance of food and high level of security – marshy wetlands discourage four-footed predators. The Danube Delta and the Camargue in France are examples of European wetlands.

Internationally, wetlands are especially important for migratory birds which breed in one continent and winter in another. Turkey, for example, has about 10,000sq km of wetlands which are important wintering areas for ducks, geese and other birds coming from their breeding grounds on the Russian tundra, or used as stopovers by those flying on into Africa.

Wasting our rivers and lakes

Many industries generate immense quantities of waste materials. Often the easiest way to get rid of these is to pour them into the nearest river. The Rhine, for instance, has been called Europe's main sewer.

Pollution has caused many rivers and lakes – including the Great Lakes of North America – to become biologically dead. One of the best known examples is America's Lake Erie. For many years sewage and industrial wastes, as well as large amounts of nitrates from fertilizers used on nearby agricultural land, were poured into the lake until it was no longer capable of supporting any type of life.

> If the level of pollution in the Rhine continues unchanged and the cumulative burden thereby continues to rise, we fear that irrepairable damage to the entire North Sea ecosystem may be inevitable.
>
> Albert Prombst
> West German Research
> Ministry

An accident at a Swiss chemical plant in 1986 resulted in a large quantity of poisonous chemicals being poured into the Rhine. This pollution of Europe's waterways threatened neighbouring countries through which the Rhine flows and was a major setback to the years of work which had gone into efforts to clean up this great river. The photograph shows eels killed by the spillage.

River estuaries, and, in tropical areas, mangrove swamps, are important habitats for many species of fish. The fish use them as spawning grounds and nurseries. But all over the world these aquatic habitats are being degraded or destroyed by industrial and agricultural pollution and the cutting of mangroves for fuel or building material. Dredging or in-filling to provide sites for buildings, roads and airports, for example, can have a devastating impact on both freshwater and coastal ecosystems. The construction of dams drowns the habitat of some species and blocks the passage of migratory fish such as the salmon.

▽ Pollution from a nearby industrial plant threatens Kenya's Lake Nakuru and its immense concentrations of flamingoes which have been described as the finest bird spectacle in the world.

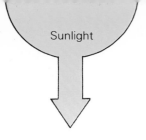

Sunlight

The ocean dump

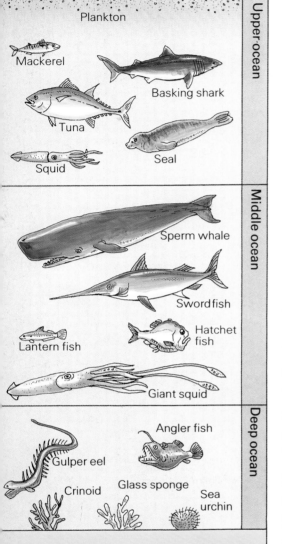

Upper ocean

Plankton
Mackerel
Basking shark
Tuna
Seal
Squid

Middle ocean

Sperm whale
Swordfish
Lantern fish
Hatchet fish
Giant squid

Deep ocean

Angler fish
Gulper eel
Crinoid
Glass sponge
Sea urchin

The seas have long been treated as the world's rubbish bin, a convenient dumping ground for all kinds of waste materials. This did not matter too much until modern industry started generating quantities of poisonous wastes which were too dangerous to dispose of on land. After the Second World War thousands of tonnes of unwanted poisonous gases, for example, were dumped at sea. More recently, the use of nuclear power plants has raised the problem of how to dispose of radioactive waste. Until recently the waste was simply tipped into the sea, sealed in special containers which, it was claimed, would be proof against corrosion until the contents stopped being radioactive.

However, most pollution of the seas comes from crude oil. Each year millions of tonnes of crude oil are carried across the oceans by mega-tankers. Occasionally tankers are wrecked, causing serious pollution. But most pollution is caused by washing out the ship's tanks at sea. This is done after the cargo has been discharged to dispose of the unwanted residue — and totals several million tonnes a year. Some of this waste finishes up fouling beaches and shore lines and causes long-term problems for ocean wildlife.

△ Plankton forms the base of the ocean food chain. It supports large numbers of small fish. These are preyed upon by larger fish, which are in turn the prey of still larger fish. Waters beneath the surface are inhabited by free-swimming fish, squids and octopuses, sharks and rays, as well as whales and dolphins.

▷ Coral reefs are formed from the skeletons of millions of tiny creatures. They are complex communities of living creatures. These range from algae to shrimps and sea slugs, and from crabs, giant clams and octopuses to many types of brilliantly coloured fish all in a balanced ecosystem. Coral formations all over the world are endangered by pollution as well as by removal of the coral for building material or for sale as tourist souvenirs. The photograph on the right contrasts a healthy reef with one that has been destroyed.

Islands - a delicate balance

The problems facing Mauritius are similar to those of many of the world's islands. When Europeans occupied Mauritius in 1598 they immediately began to exploit its natural wealth, especially the ebony forests. They brought with them goats, sheep and rabbits which destroyed the natural vegetation. Dogs and cats attacked the flightless birds such as the dodo; rats and pigs ate the eggs and hatchlings of ground-nesting birds, tortoises and turtles. Many species became extinct.

Today, Mauritius has one of the densest populations in the world. With little hope of finding employment or of leaving the island, the outlook for most of the islanders is bleak. Every available piece of land is cultivated: little of the natural habitat remains. And despite a world sugar surplus, great efforts are made to increase sugar production still more.

▽ The island of Madagascar contains plants and animals which are not found anywhere else. The aye-aye occurs only in Madagascar's rain forest. And with nine-tenths of its habitat already destroyed, it is one of the rarest animals in the world. In 1967, in an attempt to save the species from extinction, some of the last surviving aye-ayes were caught and released on the tiny uninhabited island of Nossi Mangabe, in the Bay of Antongil, where they are believed to be breeding satisfactorily.

Sugar cane plantations dominate the landscape in Mauritius. Sugar cane is easy to grow and is the mainstay of the island's economy. The only native woodlands remaining are a few isolated patches on the tops of hills. Flightless birds, such as the dodo, are characteristic of island faunas. But only one species has survived in the Indian Ocean — a flightless rail on Aldabra Atoll.

The development of commercial air routes has involved the building of airfields on previously inaccessible islands. Islands are also being used as satellite tracking stations, military bases and testing grounds for nuclear weapons. France has already carried out more than 80 nuclear tests in the Pacific. These developments, together with mass tourism and the widespread introduction of plantation crops such as sugar cane and coconut, have had catastrophic effects on many islands habitats.

"Madagascar is a microcosm of the problems facing conservationists all over the world. The remaining wild areas represent an important part of the life support system for the human population as well as the wild species."

Lee Talbot
Director General
International Union
for the Conservation
of Nature and Natural
Resources

Price of progress

On the toad tunnel plaque:

UK FIRST TOAD TUNNEL
HAMBLEDON
OPENED
FRIDAY 13TH MARCH 1987
BY
LORD SKELMERSDALE
THE TUNNEL WAS DEVELOPED BY
A PARTNERSHIP BETWEEN
ACO POLYMER PRODUCTS LTD
AND
THE FAUNA AND FLORA PRESERVATION
SOCIETY.

ACO

△ Following the country code helps to preserve the habitat

The patchwork of small fields which forms a traditional country landscape is undergoing dramatic change. In England, for example, most of the chalk downland has gone under the plough. Ponds have been filled in and fens either drained or polluted with fertilizers. The process of converting small fields into large open spaces suitable for modern farming has destroyed a quarter of the country's hedgerows. Hedgerows form strips of natural habitat, making them havens for wild flowers, butterflies, birds such as the blackbird and robin, and small mammals like the hedgehog.

◁ In the spring toads migrate to their breeding ponds. Nothing — not even a motorway — will stop them in their journey. Without specially built underpasses many would be killed by passing vehicles.

Industrial and other forms of development have had a major impact on the English landscape. Reservoirs and open-cast mining, electricity pylons and nuclear power stations, early warning systems and military training areas are some of the developments that have been imposed on the countryside. Rail and road networks, and especially motorways, take up an enormous amount of land. Roadside verges, on the other hand, have a function similar to hedgerows and, for that matter, canal and river banks. They, too, serve as wildlife sanctuaries — as long as they are not sprayed with pesticides or herbicides. The establishment of national parks is one of the main ways of preserving all types of natural habitat. In Britain, the United States and many other countries development is carefully controlled to ensure that progress does not mean the degradation or destruction of habitat and wildlife.

△ The harvestmouse is just one of the many mammals affected by the changing countryside. Everyone can help preserve the countryside by observing the country code: always obtain permission before entering private land; keep to the footpaths and close all farm gates; avoid disturbing birds' nests or touching eggs. If you want to watch a nest, do so through binoculars from a distance; do not pick wild flowers: leave them for others to enjoy; take your litter home, and leave the countryside as tidy as you would like to find it.

Hard facts

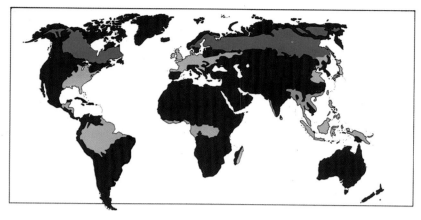

Coniferous forest

Deciduous forest

Rain forest

Coniferous forests reach across North America and Eurasia; deciduous forests occur mainly in North America and Europe, and tropical rain forests mainly in Central and South America.

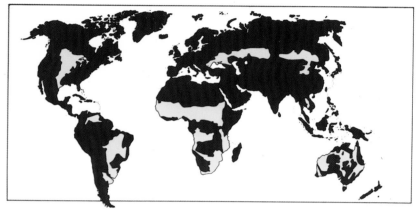

 Grasslands

The world's major grassland regions are the prairielands of North America; the pampas and chaco of South America; the Eurasian steppes; and the African savannas. All have been exploited by man.

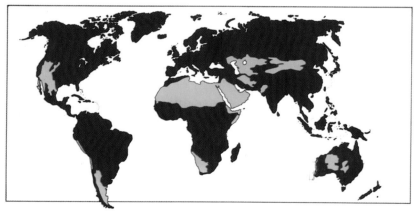

 Deserts

About one third of the world's land surface is desert. The largest and hottest is the Sahara, which occupies the greater part of northern Africa and forms part of a belt of arid lands extending across Asia to the Gobi in Mongolia.

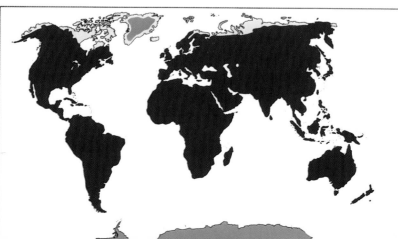

Tundra

Ice caps

The Arctic is an ice-bound ocean. Antarctica is a continental land mass buried under ice. The tundra extends through northern Canada and the USSR.

Australia

A report by the government gives particulars of widespread and increasing damage to the environment. Two thirds of the country's tree cover has been destroyed; more than half the agricultural land is affected by soil erosion; and, many rivers, wetlands and underground water sources badly degraded.

Brazil

Deforestation has reduced Brazil's Atlantic coastal forest to two per cent of its original size. This is the home of the golden lion marmoset, only about 400 of which survive.

Canada

Fears have been expressed that unless acid rain originating from industrial areas in the United States is effectively controlled, the country's maple trees will all be destroyed in 50 years time.

Chile

The Juan Fernandez Islands, off the west coast of Chile, were the setting for the story of Robinson Crusoe. Of the 97 species of plants found only on this group of islands, more than half are under threat of extinction, arising from the introduction of goats, sheep, pigs and rabbits. Overgrazing has caused serious erosion: deep gulleys are down to bedrock in many places.

China

The habitat of the giant panda in the forests of Sichuan has been seriously affected by timber extraction and grazing by domestic livestock. The Chinese authorities have taken a number of steps to safeguard the species, chief among them being the establishment of 12 special panda reserves totalling 6,000 sq km.

Indonesia

In an attempt to resolve its population problem the government is moving large numbers of people from the over-crowded islands of Java, Bali and Madura to the forests of Sumatra, Kalimantan and other outlying islands. This will inevitably be harmful to some of the most important tropical forests in the world.

Poland

The Bialowieza Forest, on the border between Poland and the USSR, is one of the last remaining areas of natural deciduous forest in Euorpe. It is the home of the only surviving herd of European bison, or wisent. At one time widespread in the temperate forests of Europe, the wisent is a woodland species and a browser, in contrast with the American bison which is a grazer. Wisent have also been reintroduced into the Caucasus.

Uganda

The mountain gorilla occupies a very restricted habitat in the mountains at the point where the borders of Zaire, Rwanda and Uganda meet. The forest habitat is constantly shrinking as more is taken over for growing crops, herding cattle and for wood cutting.

USSR

The USSR has set aside huge areas of land as nature reserves covering important types of ecosystems. Plans are being made to increase the number of reserves to include all the major types of habitat in the USSR.

United Kingdom

The merlin, Britain's smallest bird of prey, is endangered by pesticides in its food chain. Numbers (estimated at 600 pairs) are also falling because much of its moorland habitat is either being ploughed to grow crops or planted with conifers.

United States

Atlantic salmon are reported to have returned to White River, Vermont, after an absence of many years. This follows a ten year restoration programme designed to improve the quality of the water and to instal fish ladders in dams. Salmon disappeared from New England rivers a century ago.

Index

Photographic Credits:
Cover and pages 7 (bottom) and 18-19:
Survival Anglia; pages 4 (left) and back cover:
Panos Pictures; pages 4 (right), 6, 7 (top), 8,
9 (top), 13, 17 (both), 20, 26 and 27: Bruce
Coleman; pages 9 (bottom), 16, 17 (top) and
21: Zefa; pages 10-11 and 14: Spectrum; page
15: Frank Lane; page 19: Robert Harding;
pages 23 (both) and 25: Planet Earth; page 24:
John Hillelson Agency; page 28 (left): Guardian
Newspaper; page 28-29: Hutchison Library;
page 29: Tony Stone Associates.